Romantic Island Getaways

The Caribbean, Bermuda, and the Bahamas

Larry Fox
Barbara Radin-Fox

John Wiley & Sons, Inc.
New York • Chichester • Brisbane • Toronto • Singapore

Published by John Wiley & Sons, Inc.

Library of Congress Cataloging-in-Publication Data
Fox, Larry, 1945–
Romantic island getaways: the Caribbean, Bermuda, and the Bahamas /Larry Fox, Barbara Radin-Fox.
p. cm.
Includes bibliographical references and index.
ISBN 0-471-52732-7
1. West Indies—Description and travel—1981-—Guide-books.
2. Bermuda Islands—Description and travel—1979-—Guide-books.
3. Bahamas—Description and travel—1981-—Guide-books. I. Radin-Fox, Barbara. II. Title.
F1609.F69 1990
917.2904'52—dc20

90-38117
CIP

Printed in the United States of America

91 92 10 9 8 7 6 5 4 3 2 1

We dedicate this book to our mothers,
Dorothy Fox
and
Dorothy Radin.

Acknowledgments

We gratefully thank Steve Ross and Katherine Schowalter for all their guidance and support.

CONTENTS

INTEREST INDEX vii

INTRODUCTION TO ROMANTIC ISLANDS 1

1. THE GREATER ANTILLES 5
   - The Cayman Islands 6
   - Dominican Republic 12
   - Jamaica 19
   - Puerto Rico 29

2. THE LEEWARD ISLANDS 39
   - Anguilla 41
   - Antigua 46
   - British Virgin Islands 52
   - Guadeloupe 58
   - St. Barthélemey 64
   - St. Eustatius 68
   - St. Kitts and Nevis 71
   - St. Maarten/St. Martin 78
   - U.S. Virgin Islands 84

3. THE WINDWARD ISLANDS 97
   - Barbados 98
   - Dominica 105
   - Grenada 109
   - Martinique 113
   - St. Lucia 118
   - St. Vincent and the Grenadines 123

4. **THE SOUTHERN CARIBBEAN** 129
Aruba 130
Bonaire 135
Curaçao 138
Trinidad and Tobago 142

5. **THE BAHAMAS AND THE TURKS AND CAICOS** 149
The Bahamas 151
The Turks and Caicos 158

6. **BERMUDA** 163

7. **UNDERWATER WONDERS** 173

8. **FIVE SPECIAL CRUISE SHIPS** 185

9. **BE YOUR OWN CAPTAIN** 195

10. **A VILLA OF YOUR OWN** 203

11. **SPECIAL TOURS, SPAS, AND SCHOOLS** 213

12. **WAYS AND MEANS** 219

INDEX 225

INTEREST INDEX

Here is an index-style listing that highlights the islands and resorts to read about if you're going in pursuit of, or generally tend to take with you a particular appetite for, a specific activity. (Note that not all activities are listed; since this is after all a book on *romantic* getaways, we feel it's best to leave some activities to your imagination and discretion. Besides, romance is universal.)

RESORTS FOR GOLFERS

Chapter 1

Dominican Republic
- Casa de Campo
- Jaragua Resort Hotel

Grand Cayman
- Hyatt Regency

Jamaica
- Half Moon Club
- Jamaica, Jamaica
- Tryall Club

Puerto Rico
- Hyatt Cerromar Beach
- Hyatt Dorado Beach
- Palmas del Mar

Chapter 2

Guadeloupe
- Hamak

U.S. Virgin Islands
- The Buccaneer (St. Croix)
- Carambola Beach Resort (St. Croix)

Chapter 3

Barbados
- Sandy Lane

St. Lucia
- Cunard Hotel La Toc

Chapter 4

Tobago
- Mt. Irvine Bay Hotel

Chapter 5

Bahamas
- Xanadu Beach & Marine Resort
- Cotton Bay Club

Chapter 6

Bermuda
- Horizons and Cottages
- Marriott's Castle Harbour Resort
- The Princess
- Southampton Princess

RESORTS FOR HORSEBACK RIDING

Chapter 1

Dominican Republic
- Bavaro Beach Resort
- Casa de Campo
- Dorado Naco
- Playa Chiquita

Jamaica
Hedonism II
Jamaica, Jamaica

Puerto Rico
Hyatt Cerromar Beach
Hyatt Dorado Beach
Palmas del Mar

Chapter 2

Antigua
St. James Club

British Virgin Islands
Peter Island Yacht Club

Nevis
Montpelier Plantation Inn

U.S. Virgin Islands
The Buccaneer (St. Croix)

Chapter 3

Barbados
Crane Beach Hotel

St. Lucia
St. Vincent

Chapter 4

Bonaire
Curaçao
Trinidad
Tobago

Chapter 5

Abacos
Andros
Eluthera
Grand Bahama
New Providence
Turks and Caicos

Chapter 6

Bermuda

ISLANDS FOR SCUBA AND SNORKELING
(See Chapter 7)

Chapter 1

Grand Cayman

Chapter 2

Anguilla
Antigua
British Virgin Islands
Nevis
St. Croix
St. Eustatius
St. John

Chapter 3

Barbados
Grenada
Grenadines

ISLANDS FOR CASINOS

Chapter 1

Dominican Republic
Puerto Rico

Chapter 2

Guadeloupe
St. Maarten

Chapter 3

Martinique

Chapter 4

Aruba
Curaçao

Chapter 5

Bahamas

Chapter 6

Bermuda

ISLANDS FOR GLITTERING NIGHTLIFE

Chapter 1
Dominican Republic
Puerto Rico

Chapter 5
Paradise Island

ISLANDS FOR WONDERS OF NATURE

Chapter 1
Dominican Republic
Jamaica
Puerto Rico

Chapter 2
British Virgin Islands
Guadeloupe
St. Kitts
St. Maarten/St. Martin
U.S. Virgin Islands

Chapter 3
Dominica
Grenada
Martinique
St. Lucia

Chapter 4
Bonaire
Trinidad
Tobago

QUIET ISLANDS

Chapter 1
The Caymans

Chapter 2
Anguilla
British Virgin Islands
St. Barthélemy
St. Eustatius
St. Kitts and Nevis
St. John

Chapter 3
Dominica
Grenadines
Grenada
St. Lucia
St. Vincent

Chapter 4
Bonaire
Tobago

Chapter 5
The Out Islands
Turks and Caicos

TENNIS

Almost all of the resorts listed in this book have tennis courts.

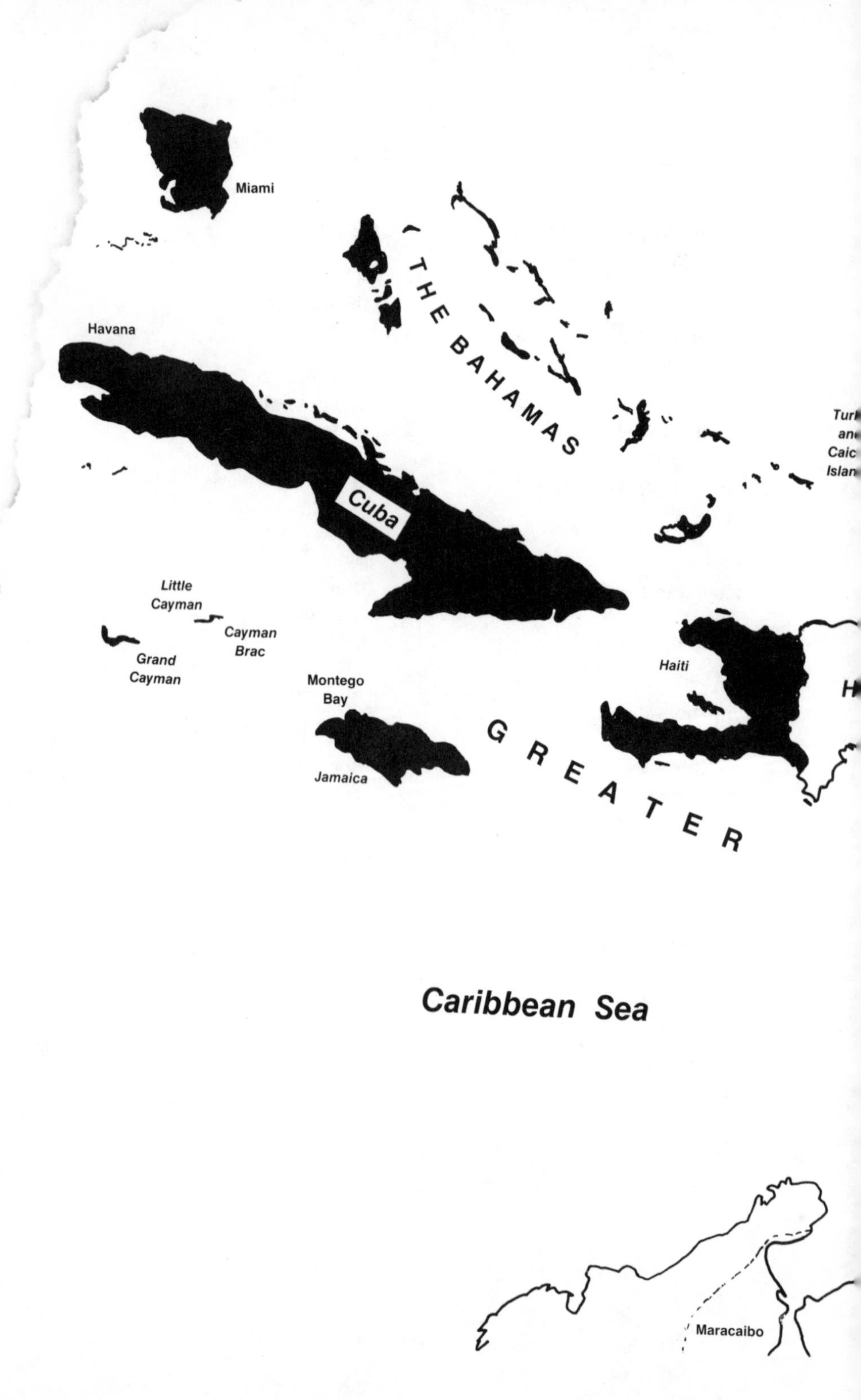

Miami
THE BAHAMAS
Havana
Cuba
Turks and Caicos Islands
Little Cayman
Cayman Brac
Grand Cayman
Montego Bay
Jamaica
Haiti
GREATER
Caribbean Sea
Maracaibo

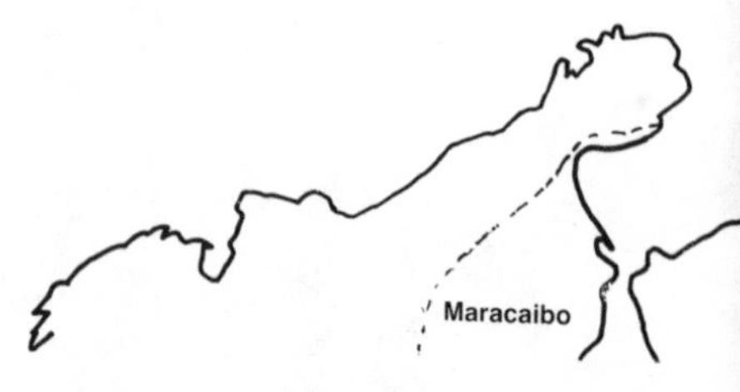

ATLANTIC OCEAN

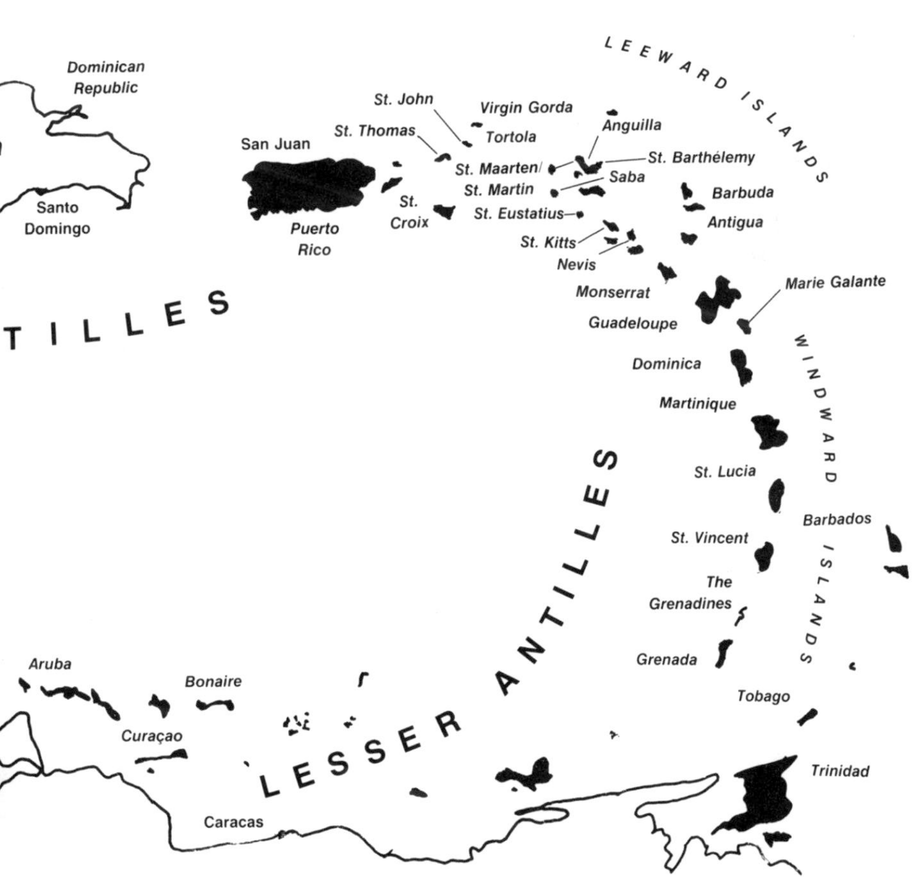

Introduction to Romantic Islands

THE ISLANDS OF THE Atlantic and Caribbean have lured us for decades with the promise that on their shores we would find all the elements needed for romance: unspoiled beaches; exotic vegetation; and skies that fill with pinks, purples, and reds at sunset, and glow with more stars than we ever imagined at night.

On Bermuda, the Bahamas, and the numerous islands of the Caribbean, we found many romantic destinations and attractions. We discovered places whose charm was their elegant simplicity and other retreats where the spell cast was simply elegant.

We found special beaches—sands of pristine white, delicate pink and peach, and muted grays—where two could find serenity. Inland, we found majestic plantation homes filled with legends of love and murder, and gardens of colorful blossoms, strange trees and flowering vines. Also, we discovered picturesque waterfalls, giant caverns, thermal springs, and huge boulders that formed grottoes at the surf's edge.

Surrounding these peaceful island attractions, in the clear and gentle seas, are the reefs and coves where a new world awaits those willing to take a look below.

What we offer in this guide are those islands, resorts, inns, restaurants, and other attractions that we believe can weave a spell of wonder for you. We also have included chapters on five special cruise ships; where to charter your own sailboat and captain; schools and dive shops that will show you underwater delights; how to rent a fabulous oceanfront villa; and, for travellers seeking something more than just sun and surf, the tour groups, schools, spas, and other places offering a potpourri of activities. A final chapter serves up information on visas, passports, currency, island transportation, health concerns, language, and other tidbits you'll need to know before you go.

First, before you continue on to the descriptions of these places, an understanding of the geography is useful.

Bermuda, of course, is a popular island destination located in the Atlantic about 600 miles due east of Cape Hatteras, North Carolina.

The Bahamas is a chain of about 700 islands—most of them tiny and uninhabited—that begins about 50 miles east of Miami and curves southeast 750 miles to just north of the Windward Passage between Cuba and Hispaniola. The Bahamas are in the Atlantic, not the Caribbean as many visitors believe. One island group often believed to be in the Caribbean—the Turks and Caicos—is actually part of the Bahamas chain and will be listed under that heading.

The Caribbean islands can be subdivided as follows:

- The *Greater Antilles*—comprised of the large islands of Jamaica, the Dominican Republic, and Puerto Rico, and the smaller Cayman Islands. (Haiti, which shares the island of Hispaniola with the Dominican Republic, and Cuba are both part of the Greater Antilles, but are not included in this guide because of the political conditions on those islands.)

- The *Lesser Antilles*—made of three subgroups. The first, the Leeward Islands, begins at the U.S. and British Virgin Islands and curves south. The Leewards also include Anguilla, St. Maarten/St. Martin, St. Barthélemy, St. Eustatius, St. Kitts, Nevis, Antigua, and Guadeloupe. (Montserrat, also part of the Leewards, was so heavily damaged by Hurricane Hugo that we have not included it in this guide.)

  The second group, the Windward Islands, continue the curve south and are made up of Dominica, Martinique, St. Lucia, Barbados, St. Vincent and the Grenadines, and Grenada.

  The final group is made of those islands in the Southern Caribbean. These islands include three called the Netherlands Antilles—Aruba, Bonaire and Curaçao—plus Trinidad and Tobago.

These islands are very different, sharing only the sea and sun. They range in size from less than 10 square miles to more than a thousand times that. Their cultures are the present-day synthesis of many from the past: Indian, African, Spanish, French, Dutch, British, and American.

We first began to appreciate just how romantic an island could be on our honeymoon, when we sat on the terrace at a 200-year-old inn listening to a pianist while we looked down at the harbor of Charlotte Amalie on St. Thomas. Below us, a restless movement of lights—on land and on the water of the harbor and the shimmering Caribbean—created a show that conjured up visions of adventure and excitement.

There have been many other islands and many other romantic moments, but for as long as we live, the memory of that particular romantic journey remains alive in our hearts.

What more could we ask?

LARRY FOX
BARBARA RADIN-FOX

The Su Casa restaurant, located in a Spanish colonial mansion, at the Hyatt Dorado Beach resort on Puerto Rico. (*Photo Courtesy of the Hyatt Dorado*.)

CHAPTER 1

The Greater Antilles

THE GREATER ANTILLES, made up of three large islands (Jamaica, the Dominican Republic, and Puerto Rico) and one small island group (the Caymans), offers a broad diversity of geography and diversions. On these islands you will find some of the finest beaches in the Caribbean; mountainous interiors where caves, rivers, and waterfalls beckon; and diving and snorkeling that is the best in the region and among the most exciting in the world.

The big islands are also known for their golf resorts, fabulous nightlife, and historical towns with buildings that date back to the sixteenth and seventeenth centuries.

The Greater Antilles Islands host two cultures, English and Spanish. Each played a dominant role in the European colonization of the Caribbean.

THE CAYMAN ISLANDS

Lying 180 miles west-northwest of Jamaica, this British Crown Colony is known for its prosperous economy and scores of offshore banks that cater to clients who wish to keep their banking secret. For those not interested in economics, however, the three flat islands that make up the Caymans offer spotless and uncrowded beaches and some of the world's finest diving and snorkeling.

On Grand Cayman, the largest of the three islands (28 by 7 miles), is the capital of George Town. George Town is a small, attractive, low-key town, famed for its duty-free shops and two museums—the Cayman Maritime and Treasure Museum and the McKee's Treasure Museum—that display some of the artifacts and relics recovered from the numerous shipwrecks in the area.

George Town is also the site every October of "Pirate's Week," a week-long festival celebrating the buccaneer Blackbeard and his naughty nautical deeds. A mock pirate invasion, parade, golf tournament, and other activities take place during the festival. Visit the tourism office on North Church Street and pick up maps and brochures on these and other attractions.

Grand Cayman is also home to some of the Caribbean's finest shores. Seven Mile Beach (the name is a misnomer; it's not even six miles long) is a pristine stretch of white sand that is home to many of the island's resorts. The other top beaches on Grand Cayman are at East End, Cayman Kai, and Rum Point.

The other two Cayman Islands, Little Cayman (10 square miles) and Cayman Brac (14 square miles), are long and skinny spits of land about 80 miles east-northeast of the large island. These two tiny islands offer a few uncrowded beaches and numerous opportunities for bird-watching, fishing, diving, and snorkeling.

The real attraction in the Caymans is underwater, where the slopes of the mountains that created the islands offer absolutely stunning views of marine life, shipwrecks, and undersea caves in water so clear you can often see as far as 200 feet.

Diving in the Caymans is for both the novice and the expert, with numerous schools, dive shops, and boats available to teach beginners or to take the more experienced hands off to deeper and more adventurous locations. Lessons and trips can be arranged at your hotel.

Much of the diving off Grand Cayman takes place off the west coast, where a marine park is a haven for divers. The huge North Sound, where it looks like a giant took a bite out of the island, and Rum Point, the eastern tip of the sound, are also popular with the underwater set. Take time to stop in Batabano, where the fishermen bring in their catch. The east end of the island is where divers find the Wall, a sharp dropoff that is a magnet for marine life. Other East End attractions include Bodden Town, the Cayman's first capital; the famed blow holes where surf shoots skyward through holes in the coral; and several wrecks that are visible from the shore.

For experienced divers, Little Cayman offers the Bloody Bay Wall, a 6,000-foot underwater dropoff that offers sights rarely seen by undersea explorers. Visitors can get to Cayman Brac and Little Cayman on Cayman Airways (800/422-9696).

Finally, if you prefer your underwater experiences on the dry side, you can take a one-hour underwater cruise on a sightseeing submarine and test the deeper waters in a two-passenger research sub. The sightseeing submarine *Atlantis* offers day and night cruises for $48 to $57 (809/949-7700); a 75-minute dive to deep water on the Research Submersibles costs about $250 per passenger (809/949-8296).

For more information about scuba and snorkeling schools and other water sports in the Caymans, please read Chapter 7, "Underwater Wonders."

Romantic Retreats

The Caymans are a popular resort in the winter months. Plan to book several months ahead and also expect to pay top rates. There are few bargains on these islands.

The rates are for a room for two per night and do not include meals unless noted. The three categories:

Inexpensive—Less than $100
Expensive—$100 to $200
Very expensive—$200 and more

Meal plans are offered at many hotels and can help cut costs. All-inclusive plans offer all meals, snacks, drinks, wine, entertainment, activities, sports, gratuities, and airport transfers for one fee, which ranges from $1,000 to $3,000 per person per week. Whether that is a bargain depends on how much you eat, drink, and play and whether you want more freedom to sample restaurants elsewhere on the island. Ask your travel agent for current tariffs and the all-inclusive and other meal plans.

Our favorites on Grand Cayman

Caribbean Club. This beachfront resort has 18 villas, with one or two bedrooms and kitchen facilities, tennis courts, and water sports. Casual, but pleasantly quiet. Expensive/very expensive. 809/947-4099 or 800/327-8777.

Cayman Kai. The 26 sea lodges at this oceanfront resort are striking; the white-peaked roofs make it look like a campground for the super-rich. Each lodge has a complete kitchen and either one or two bedrooms. Larger units are available in townhouses and beach cottages. Stick with the sea lodges. This resort is made for the diver. It's on the north coast and has a complete dive shop offering rentals, lessons, and guided dives. Other activities include fishing, water sports, and tennis. Expensive. 809/947-9556 or 800/223-5427.

Hyatt Regency Grand Cayman. The finest of the Cayman resorts, this lavish 279-room hotel across from the Seven Mile Beach offers spacious rooms with such luxurious appointments as verandas, over-size tubs, and elegant furnishings. Sports facilities include the only golf course on the island, a pool, tennis courts, a marina, and water sports facilities. Very expensive. 809/949-1234 or 800/553-1300.

Treasure Island Resort. This activity-filled resort emphasizes sports and evening entertainment. The latter shouldn't surprise you, for Treasure Island is owned by country stars Larry Gatlin, Randy Travis, and other musicians of note. There are 290 rooms, all colorfully decorated and with a view of the shore or pool. Facilities include tennis courts and water sports facilities. Very expensive. 809/949-7777 or 800/874-0027.

On Cayman Brac:

Tiara Beach Resort. This is a diver's resort, offering a bluff-top location on the small island and the Peter Hughes Dive Center, where everything for the diver can be bought, rented, or arranged. There are 76 rooms in the three-story buildings, all tastefully furnished. Other activities and facilities include all forms of water sports, tennis, a pool, and the beach. The food is mediocre, but the divers don't seem to mind. Very expensive. 809/948-7553 or 800/367-3484.

On Little Cayman:

Southern Cross Club. Another diver's resort, this 24-room all-inclusive resort offers great diving and comfortable, but not elegant, accommodations. Complete dive and water sports facilities. Expensive. 809/948-3255 or 317/636-9501.

For information about homes that you can rent in the Caymans, please read Chapter 10, "A Villa of Your Own."

Dining and Nightlife

The best dining in the Caymans is found in the bigger resorts. Call for reservations and check the dress code. It may be the Caribbean, but some places require a jacket and tie.

The following price categories for restaurants are for dinner for two, without wine or alcoholic beverages:

Inexpensive—$30 and less
Moderate—$30 to $50
Expensive—$50 to $100
Very expensive—More than $100

All of our recommended restaurants are on Grand Cayman:

Caribbean Club. A continental menu, but stick with the seafood and be patient with the service. Expensive. Jacket and tie required. 809/947-4099.

Chef Tell's Grand Old House. The television chef ("very simple, very easy") mixes his continental creations with some popular local seafood dishes. His creations are best. Superb service, elegant Victorian decor. Great for romance. Expensive. 809/949-2020.

The Cook Rum. This West Indian spot offers very casual decor but some of the finest of the local fare. Try the pepper pot stew, turtle stew, and salt beef. Inexpensive. 809/949-8670.

L'Escargot. The setting is elegant: crystal, silver, tuxedoed waiters, and live piano music; but this sometimes overwhelms the quality of the food at this Treasure Island Resort dining room. The whole package is romantic, though. The French menu features escargot in more forms than we thought existed. Jacket and tie required. Expensive. 809/949-7255.

Ristorante Pappagallo. If you want to get away from the city and resort crowds, head out to Spanish Cove and dine in this funky, casual, thatched-roof restaurant with caged macaws and a northern Italian menu. The food is good and a welcome change from the continental/seafood menus elsewhere. Expensive. Call for directions. 809/949-3479.

Nightlife on the Caymans is limited. The big resorts offer their version of a nightclub with house and island bands. The best is Silver's

Nightclub, in the Treasure Island Resort. Here a house band plays a bit of everything from reggae to rock to country. For the current report on "what" is playing "where," pick up a copy of the free local paper, *Cayman After Dark*.

For more information contact the Cayman Islands Department of Tourism, 250 Catalonia Ave., Suite 604, Coral Gables, FL 33134, or call them at 305/444-6551. In the Caymans, the tourism office is located in the Tower Building, North Church Street, George Town, 809/949-7999.

DOMINICAN REPUBLIC

Columbus was the first tourist to visit the island of Hispaniola. During his epic voyage in 1492, he wrecked his ship *Santa Maria* on the Atlantic shore. The island captivated the explorer despite his misfortune, for Columbus named the island *La Isla Espanola* and called it "the most beautiful land human eyes have ever seen."

After establishing an ill-fated outpost on the island, Columbus sailed back to Spain. He returned a year later to create a second, more successful settlement, governed by his brother Bartholomew. In 1496, Bartholomew founded another town, Santo Domingo, which in time became the center of Spanish influence in the New World.

Today, the island of Hispaniola is divided. Two-thirds (18,800 square miles) is the Dominican Republic; the western third is Haiti, a country beset by poverty and political turmoil.

The Dominican Republic boasts political stability; more than 1,000 miles of fine beaches; numerous luxury hotels and resorts; fine golf courses; a capital with a magnificent sixteenth-century old section; the highest mountain in the West Indies; and offshore wonders that include sunken ships, reefs filled with sea life, and an annual visit by humpback whales.

Santo Domingo, on the south coast, is like San Juan in Puerto Rico; a capital city with two faces, one very old and the other very new. Santo Domingo has a 12-block area called the Colonial Zone. This historic area offering narrow crowded streets, historic old buildings, shops, and interesting and innovative restaurants. Before you take a walking tour, visit the Tourist Information Center on Avenida George Washington and pick up a map and other guides or call 809/682-8181.

The best place to start a tour of the old city is at Columbus Square, or Parque Colón. On the south side of the square is the Catedral Menor de Santa María, whose construction started in 1514. There are those who argue that the bronze and marble sarcophagus within holds the remains of Christopher Columbus. In 1877, during work in the cathedral, an urn bearing the inscription "the illustrious baron Don Cristóbal Colón, first admiral of America" was discovered. Inscription or not, scholars are not convinced that the urn holds the remains of Columbus.

Other nearby historic sights include the ruins of the Hospital de San Nicolás de Bari on Calle Hosta, the first hospital in the New World; the nearby ruins of the San Francisco Monastery that was built in 1512; and, on the Calle Emiliano Tejera, the Casa del Cordon, the oldest surviving house (1503).

Historic buildings are not the only attraction. On the Calle Las Damas, said to be the New World's oldest street, you will find the Museo de las Casas Reales (Museum of the Royal Houses), two sixteenth-century houses now exhibiting antique coins, relics, armor, furniture, and Indian artifacts, and Alcázar de Colón, the castle of Don Diego Colón, son of the admiral and viceroy of the island.

The Colonial Zone is also home to many fine shops. La Atarazana and El Mercada Modelo are home to shops selling fine art, jewelry, and fashion. The main shopping streets are Calle Duarte and Calle El Conde.

At night, take a stroll along the Malecón, the seafront promenade, and enjoy another national treasure. *Merengue*, both the sensual music and the dance, can be enjoyed at many of the area's nightclubs, taverns, and restaurants. Merengue is almost as common as the fabrics and designer clothing of Oscar de la Renta, whose creations can be seen almost everywhere.

One other sight you shouldn't miss while in Santo Domingo is the Jardín Botanico Nacional, just north of town. You can tour its 445 acres by train or horse-drawn carriage. The sights include a large display of orchids, a gorgeous Japanese garden, and a large floral clock display.

With 1,000 miles of beaches, it's hard to choose just where to sun yourself. Boca Chica, 21 miles outside the capital, is a well-known spot, but it's too crowded. Instead, on the south coast, try Juan Dolio; on the eastern tip, try the 20-mile-long Punta Cana; and on the north shore, visit Playa Grande, Sosúa, the famous Puerto Plata, and Luperón Beach. While these and many others are fine, the beach at your resort may be just as good.

Inland attractions include the Parque de Los Tres Ojos (Park of Three Eyes) on La Romana, about two hours east of the capital on the southern shore. The "eyes" are blue mini-lagoons that peer out of limestone caverns. A few minutes' drive east, in Altos de Chavón, is a replica of a medieval Spanish village. The village is nice, but it is the artists who live and work there who make this a special place.

The highest peak of the island's two mountain ranges is Pico Duarte, which rises 10,414 feet. The mountain roads that connect the south shore with the north are scenic, taking you past plantations, beautiful valleys, waterfalls, and rivers.

The main attraction on the north shore is Puerto Plata, a booming resort town combining the best of Victorian architecture with the worst of concrete engineering. Don't miss the Museum of Dominican Amber on Calle Duarte, which showcases jewelry and other items made from the large deposits of amber found on the north coast. These deposits gave the northwest coast the name "Amber Coast."

The waters of the northern coast are also the winter home of the humpback whales, who migrate there from the icy waters of Iceland, Greenland, and North America. The whales can be spotted in the Silver Banks, an area in the Atlantic about 80 miles northeast of Puerto Plata, and in the Samana Bay about two hours east of the resort town.

The most spectacular view on the island is from the north coast's Mt. Isabel de Terres, a modest peak (2,600 feet), but one which you can reach by cable car. From the garden on top, the Atlantic Ocean seems to roll into eternity.

Romantic Retreats

The Dominican Republic is famous for its lavish resorts, many offering every conceivable sports activity.

The rates are for a room for two per night and do not include meals unless noted. The three categories:

Inexpensive—Less than $100
Expensive—$100 to $200
Very expensive—$200 and more

Meal plans are offered at many hotels and can help cut costs. All-inclusive plans offer all meals, snacks, drinks, wine, entertainment, activities, sports, gratuities, and airport transfers for one fee, which ranges from $1,000 to $3,000 per person per week. Whether that is a bargain depends on how much you eat, drink, and play and whether you want more freedom to sample restaurants elsewhere on the island. Check your travel agent for current tariffs and the all-inclusive and other meal plans.

Our favorites in and near Santo Domingo:

Hotel Santo Domingo. Decorated by Oscar de la Renta, this chic 220-room hotel is bright, spacious, and very elegant. Facilities include sun deck, sauna, three tennis courts, and a pool. Expensive. 809/532-1511 or 800/223-6620.

Jaragua Resort Hotel, Casino, and European Spa. This hotel offers everything: a stunning location, waterfalls, gardens, 355 spacious and fully-equipped rooms, top entertainers in the large nightclub, a casino, and a staff doctor to supervise your diet. Other amenities include a beautiful pool, five tennis courts, a golf course, and spa with exercise and diet programs, saunas, and whirlpool. Expensive. 809/685-4151 or 800/223-9815; in Canada, 8700/468-0023.

Hostal Nicolás de Ovando. The oldest hotel in the New World, this 60-room establishment was home to the first island governor in the sixteenth century. The decor is Spanish: dark carved woods, tapestries, beams, and arches. Inexpensive. 809/687-3101.

On the Amber Coast:

Dorado Naco. This is a complex of one- and two-bedroom villas, 202 rooms in all. There is an organized schedule of activities for guests. Facilities include pool, a water sports center, and beach; horseback riding and bicycle rentals are also available. Expensive. 809/586-2019 or 800/322-2388.

Playa Chiquita. The 90 suites in this Sosúa resort offer colorful and comfortable accommodations, a small beach, and a serene atmosphere. Facilities include pool, horseback riding, and water sports. Expensive. 809/689-6191.

On the Eastern Coast:

Bavaro Beach Resort. The rooms are comfortable but not exceptional at this resort, whose main attraction is the 20 miles of pristine beach in front of the hotel. The five buildings hold 1,000 rooms, a bit too large for our taste, but then there is that beach. . . . Facilities include two pools, tennis courts, horseback riding, and water sports. Expensive. 809/682-2162.

On the Southern Coast:

Casa de Campo. The real jewel of the island is this stunning 7,000-acre resort that offers beautifully landscaped grounds, 350 rooms, suites, and villas from one to three bedrooms, and condominium apartments. There are 13 tennis courts, two golf courses, polo fields, countless horses, eight restaurants, and endless activities. The only thing it doesn't have is a beach, but transportation to a nearby shore is free. Very expensive. 809/682-2162.

For information about homes you can rent, please read Chapter 10, "A Villa of Your Own."

Dining and Nightlife

The national dish of the Dominican Republic is *La Bandera* (The Flag), a plate of stewed beef, rice, and red beans. Don't miss *yaniqueques* (Johnny Cakes), a sweet doughy bread.

The following price categories for restaurants are for dinner for two, without wine or alcoholic beverages:

Inexpensive—$30 and less
Moderate—$30 to $50
Expensive—$50 to $100
Very expensive—More than $100

In and Near Santo Domingo:

Alcazar. Designed by Oscar de la Renta and located in the Hotel Santo Domingo, this elegant restaurant offers Moorish decor and some simply stunning seafood dishes. Expensive. 809/532-1511.

Café St. Michel. This award-winning French restaurant serves some of the finest food on the island. Moderate. 809/562-4141.

Fonda de la Atarazana. Music, dancing, and the location in the Colonial Zone make this continental restaurant a very special place. Moderate. 809/689-2900.

La Bahia. This restaurant serves some excellent Dominican dishes. Stick with the seafood. Inexpensive. 809/682-4022.

Lina. This chić restaurant offers fine continental dishes. Try the paella or the mixed seafood casserole. Expensive. 809/689-5185.

Mesón de la Cava. You've heard of underground nightspots. This certainly fits the name. It's tucked away in a natural cave 50 feet below ground; its decor includes stalactites and stalagmites. The fare is typical continental, but the location and the nightly music and dancing make this an exceptional dining spot. Expensive. 809/533-2818.

Vesuvio. The menu is Italian and the execution and the use of fresh seafood make this a superb restaurant. Expensive. 809/682-2766.

In La Romana:

Café del Sol. This small outdoor café in a sixteenth-century setting serves up fine light fare and pizza. Moderate. 809/682-9656.

In Puerto Plata:

Flamingo's. Dine outside overlooking a pool at this superb continental spot. Expensive. 809/586-2019.

Jimmy's. Try the beef at this good steakhouse. Moderate. 809/586-4325.

For nightlife, check the free publications *Touring* and *Vacation Guide,* which you can get at the tourist information offices. They carry listings of current entertainment.

The best nightclubs are in the big hotels. Try the nightspots in the Jaragua Resort and Santo Domingo Sheraton. Las Palmas in the Hotel Santo Domingo is great for dancing.

For more information contact the Dominican Tourist Information Center, 485 Madison Ave., New York, NY 10022 or call 212/826-0750. On the island there are Tourism Information Centers on Avenida George Washington (809/682-8181) and in Puerto Plata (809/586-3676). These offices can provide maps and other guides to sights.

JAMAICA

"The fairest island that eyes have beheld," said Christopher Columbus upon viewing the north coast of Jamaica in 1494.

Lush with jungle that stretches from sea to mountain, the third largest island in the Caribbean is a seductive place that enchants visitors with its beautiful beaches, cinematic sunsets, a lively culture that is a blend of English, West Indian, African and Asian, and a host of natural wonders.

The island's spell has captured many who came for a visit but stayed on forever. Writers Noel Coward and Ian Fleming made their homes here, as well as two famed swashbucklers, the real-life pirate Henry Morgan and the Hollywood buccaneer Errol Flynn.

Jamaica is 142 miles long and as much as 52 miles wide, and within its 4,411 square miles are three distinct areas. The north shore, where the beach resorts are found; Kingston, the bustling and bursting capital; and the interior, the mysterious and mountainous region rarely visited by outsiders.

For a romantic destination, head for the north shore where Columbus first felt the island's pull. There you will find magnificent beaches, hedonistic and elegant resorts, some historic towns, and some stunning waterfalls.

Port Antonio, east of Ocho Rios, was the first tourist spot on the island, attracting such notables as J. P. Morgan, Rudyard Kipling, William Randolph Hearst, and Errol Flynn. The jet-setters have gone elsewhere, but the colorful streets of Port Antonio and the stately homes that line them remain, waiting to be discovered again.

The best public beaches on the island are between Port Antonio and Negril. Doctor's Cave Beach in downtown Montego Bay is a fine stretch of sand, though development is crowding it. In Ocho Rios, the preferred public beaches are Mallard's Beach and Turtle Beach, while Port Antonio devotees swear by San San Bay. Negril's beaches are world famous, but much of the famed seven-mile-long Negril Beach is open only to guests of the resorts on the strand. For the adventurous (and those well-stocked with sun block) many of the larger resorts set aside part of their beach as swimsuit-optional or nude-only spots.

There are few resorts on the south coast, whose main attraction is Kingston, the largest English-speaking city south of Florida and home to almost one million of Jamaica's 2.4 million residents. Kingston is the capital of Jamaica and the center of politics, finance, and industry. It also is the heart and soul of Jamaican culture, art, and music. Kingston is the place to transact business or shop for art and craft items, but it is too big, too crowded, and too busy to be a romantic destination.

The scenic wonders of Jamaica are found in the less-visited interior, the home of some magnificent peaks (Blue Mountain tops out at 7,402 feet), graceful waterfalls, coffee plantations, rum distilleries, and that rarely explored area of scarred and tortured limestone called the Cockpit Country. The descendants of fugitive slaves live there, as apart from the rest of Jamaican society as they were when they fled from their slaveholders. If you have time, arrange for a tour of this region through your hotel.

The mile-high Blue Mountains near Kingston are the site of an exotic garden created in 1868. The Cinchona (the name comes from the cinchona tree, whose bark is used to make quinine) Gardens offer lovely flowers, including orchids, hydrangea, azalea, and lilies on a spectacular hillside setting. Other wonderful gardens on the island include Carinosa, where 20 acres of orchids, hibiscus, and other flowers, vines, and bushes create a magnificent attraction around a waterfall in the hills overlooking Ocho Rios; Athenry Gardens, a 185-acre garden in the hills above Port Antonio; and the Shaw Park Botanical Gardens near Ocho Rios, where you can see orchids, lilies, and a stunning banyan tree.

On most islands, off-beach diversions include shopping. However, on Jamaica, this can be a frustrating experience. Ocho Rios and Montego Bay have large craft bazaars, but the variety of items offered is limited and some visitors may not like shopping amid a crowd of pleading sellers.

Better craft items can be found at Devon House (26 Hope Road in Kingston), where fine arts and foods are sold in a building that dates back to the island's colonial era; at the Gallery of West Indian Art (1 Orange Lane in Montego Bay) for nice pottery and Jamaican and Haitian paintings; or the Coconut Grove Plaza in the center of Ocho Rios. Caribatik, two miles east of Falmouth on the north shore road, offers some stunning batik creations by resident owner/artist Muriel Chandler. Don't overlook the boutiques at the larger hotels and at the airport in Montego Bay.

Jamaica's colonial heritage and legends can be found in its great plantation houses. Rose Hall Great House, just east of Montego Bay, was the eighteenth-century home of Annie Palmer, "the White Witch of Rose Hall," who is said to have murdered her three husbands and one lover. Greenwood Great House, located 15 miles east of Montego Bay, was the home of the Barrett family (of Elizabeth Barrett Browning fame). South of Falmouth is Good Hope, a plantation and great house built by John Thorp (sometimes spelled Tharp), one of the richest planters in Jamaican history. Harmony Hall, a modest "great house" on the coast road near Ocho Rios, is a superb art gallery. All these attractions are open daily.

At night, the rivers become the sites of dinners and dancing. You can enjoy a Jamaican buffet and dancing under torchlight at White River, east of Ocho Rios, or be entertained by a floorshow while dining on the torchlit banks of the Great River near Montego Bay. Make reservations through your hotel's tour desk.

Visitors to Jamaica should not leave without seeing the magnificent Dunn's River Falls, a 600-foot staircase of water that may be the most photographed attraction on the island. The second best cascade is Somerset Falls, a 400-foot-long rush of water near Port Antonio. Both falls are gentle enough to be climbed with the assistance of a guide.

Finally, no visit to Jamaica would be complete without a late afternoon stop at Rick's Café in Negril on the west end of the island. From this vantage point, while you watch the sun set and the cliff divers take their breath-taking plunges into the water, life back home seems far, far away.

Romantic Retreats

Jamaica has some fine resorts featuring extensive sports facilities and great beaches.

The rates are for a room for two per night, and do not include meals unless noted. The three categories:

Inexpensive—Less than $100
Expensive—$100 to $200
Very expensive—$200 and more

Meal plans are offered at many hotels and can help cut costs. All-inclusive plans offer all meals, snacks, drinks, wine, entertainment, activities, sports, gratuities, and airport transfers for one fee, which ranges from $1,000 to $3,000 per person per week. Whether that is a bargain depends on how much you eat, drink, and play and whether you want more freedom to sample restaurants elsewhere on the island. Check your travel agent for current tariffs and the all-inclusive and other meal plans.

Our favorites on the island, in Montego Bay:

Half Moon Golf, Tennis & Beach Club. There are 197 rooms at this elegant resort on a curved beach just east of Montego Bay. Created by a group of millionaires who wanted their own private resort, Half Moon offers beach-front villas in a variety of sizes and styles, and luxury rooms in the main house and elsewhere on the grounds. Some of the villas have private pools. We loved everything about this elegant resort and cannot wait until we return for a longer stay. It has an 18-hole golf course designed by Robert Trent Jones, a tennis center with 13 courts (four lighted), four lighted squash courts, water sports, health club, and shopping arcade. Very expensive. The all-inclusive plan is a great bargain. 809/953-2211 and 800/237-3237.

Richmond Hill. A former mansion known for its dining room, Richmond Hill offers 23 rooms and a spectacular view from its open terrace and hilltop location overlooking the waterfront. The rooms are small but furnished with style and taste. Inexpensive. 809/952-3859.

Round Hill. Noel Coward, Cole Porter, and Irving Berlin stayed at Round Hill, and legend has it that all played the piano at this 98-acre enclave on a peninsula near Montego Bay. There are 98 rooms and suites in the main house and a number of private villas for rent. Guests have golf privileges at Tryall. Other features include a good beach, water sports, a boutique, nightly dinner dances, and a nightclub. Very expensive. An all-inclusive plan is available. 809/952-5150 and 800/237-3237.

Tryall Golf, Tennis & Beach Club. There are 44 rooms in the great house, which was built in 1834, and 40 villas of varying sizes. The atmosphere is that of an elegant, exclusive club. Facilities include a wonderful, crescent beach, 18-hole golf course, lighted tennis courts, water sports center, and 2200 acres of gardens and grounds. Very expensive. An all-inclusive plan is available and is a great saving if you are staying a week. 809/952-5110 and 800/237-3237.

Near Negril:

Charela Inn. This beachfront, Spanish-style villa offers 14 rooms in a garden setting. The guest rooms are comfortably sized and attractively furnished. The inn is known for its superb French and Jamaican cuisine. Expensive. 809/957-4277.

Grand Lido. This elegant Super Club resort, part of a small chain of all-inclusive, activity-filled resorts, offers all the amenities in one of the finest locations in the Caribbean. There are 200 rooms on a two-mile-long beach, each with a private balcony. Facilities include two pools, five jacuzzis, four tennis courts, water sports center, and a fitness center. Wonderful, but a bit too busy for our tastes. All-inclusive. 809/957-4317.

Hedonism II. This big resort (280 rooms) lives up to its name with nonstop activities, party atmosphere, nude beaches, and an extensive sports complex. Facilities include water sports, fitness center, disco, horseback riding, lighted tennis courts, and shuffleboard and volleyball courts. All-inclusive. 809/957-4200.

Sandals Negril. This new resort is actually made of parts of two older spas, the Coconut Cove and the Sundowner. There are 199 rooms, including 16 loft suites, all located on a seven-mile beach, the longest in Jamaica. Facilities and attractions include water sports, three lighted tennis courts, health club, outdoor games, recreation program, nightly entertainment, and a constant party atmosphere. All-inclusive. 809/957-4216 and 800/327-1991.

Near Ocho Rios:

Jamaica Inn. There are 50 rooms in this beachfront inn that offers a quiet retreat from the busy atmosphere of the larger resorts. Guests can use golf, tennis, and riding facilities at nearby hotels and country clubs. Expensive. 809/974-2514.

Plantation Inn. Located on a small peninsula, this colonial plantation-style inn offers a quiet and stylish retreat from the partylike atmosphere found at many Caribbean resorts. There are great views from the inn, located on a low bluff above the beach. Amenities include nightly dancing, shops, rooms with verandas, and that calming ambiance. Expensive. 809/974-2501.

Sans Souci. This pastel-pink hotel overlooking the sea is built on and down the face of a tall bluff that is covered with plush tropical plants, a waterfall, and a tiny lagoon for Charlie the Turtle. The views are simply stunning, the 80 rooms and their furnishings are widely diverse, and the spa and health club facilities will pamper you. Other facilities include a great gift shop, beach, tennis courts, a water sports center, two pools, and a lush garden setting. Very expensive. 809/974-2353 and 800/237-3237.

Near Port Antonio:

Trident Villas & Hotel. Peacocks walk the lawns, the service is impeccable, and the rugged shore offers a dramatic backdrop for this elegant resort of 16 suites and 12 villas. There is a small beach, stunning oceanfront pool, tennis courts, and a dining room known for its cuisine throughout the island. Very expensive. 809/993-2590 and 800/237-3237.

Goblin Hill. There are 28 villas on the 13 lush acres of this elegant little resort. Each villa comes with a butler and maid. Facilities include tennis courts, pool, and the nearby beach at San San Bay. There is no dining room or bar on the property. Expensive. 809/993-3049.

Near Runaway Bay:

Jamaica, Jamaica. This 152-room Super Club resort emphasizes Jamaican food, activities and culture, and a casual, please-yourself atmosphere. Activities include golf, tennis, horseback riding, water sports, nightclubbing, and more. All-inclusive. 809/973-2436.

For information about homes you can rent in Jamaica, please read Chapter 10, "A Villa of Your Own." Also note: An association of the Elegant Resorts of Jamaica—Trident Villas, Sans Souci, Jamaica Inn, Round Hill, Half Moon, and Tryall—allow guests to dine and sleep at other resorts in the association under their Platinum all-inclusive plan.

Dining and Nightlife

Dining in Jamaica offers you an opportunity to try some outstanding local dishes. The best include curried goat, saltfish and the local vegetable called ackee, the fiery jerked pork and chicken, pepperpot soup, and patties (the ubiquitous meat pies).

The following price categories for restaurants are for dinner for two, without wine or alcoholic beverages:

Inexpensive—$30 and less
Moderate—$30 to $50

Expensive—$50 to $100
Very expensive—More than $100

Jamaican Dishes: Unique and Memorable

One of the pleasures of traveling in the islands is the opportunity to sample native cuisines. In Jamaica, ackee and saltfish, curried goat, and jerk pork and chicken are some of the tantalizing local dishes that you may want to try.

Ackee and saltfish, considered by many to be the national dish of Jamaica although it appears on few restaurant menus, is a combination of salted local fish and a local vegetable, ackee, that looks and tastes a lot like scrambled eggs.

Another Jamaican favorite is curried goat, whose taste has lingered in my memory since we first tried it years ago. The curried goat is spicy, of course, and tastes much like Indian lamb curry, but we think the goat meat is much more tender. We love it, though we must admit that we feel very sad when we think of the many adorable goats that roam the island.

Jerk pork or jerk chicken is the Jamaican equivalent of barbecue. Jerk is a paste of hot peppers, berries, and other herbs in which the meat is marinated for several hours. The meat is then wrapped in foil, cooked under a fire of pimento (allspice) leaves for several hours to tenderize, and finally grilled just before serving.

After any of these dishes, enjoy wonderful Jamaican Blue coffee, which may be the best in the world.

In Montego Bay:

Georgian House. Set in two restored eighteenth-century houses, this restaurant serves up some fine continental and Jamaican dishes. Expensive. Free pickup from area hotels. 809/952-0632.

Marguerite's. Seafood is superb at this waterfront restaurant that is always crowded. Moderate. 809/952-4777.

The Sugar Mill. Dining on the open air terrace of this superb restaurant at Half Moon's golf course is a very romantic experience. The lobsters are popular, but try the Jamaican dishes. Expensive. 809/953-2650.

Town House. Favored by prominent visitors for decades, this restaurant is known for its genteel setting and superb, though uncreative, cuisine. Stick to the fish. Moderate. 809/952-2660.

The Pork Pit. The jerked pork is fiery, the beer is cold, and the ambiance—well, at this open air stand, it isn't much. Hit it for lunch. It's next to the Casa Montego Hotel. Inexpensive.

In Ocho Rios:

Casanova. In the Sans Souci Hotel, this restaurant features Italian and seafood fare. But if native dishes are among the specials, try them. Expensive. 809/974-2353.

The Ruins. It's an open air restaurant with a waterfall, lush vegetation, actual ruins, and dining areas connected by footbridges. Stick to the seafood. Expensive. 809/974-2442.

Almond Tree. Stick to the island dishes. Moderate. 809/993-2604.

In Negril:

Rick's Café. Attractions include breathtaking sunsets, rugged cliffs, and heartstopping cliffdivers. The menu reads like that at a brunch back in the states, but the scenery and sights make up for any shortcomings. Moderate. 809/957-4335.

Most nightlife in Jamaica is at the major resorts, and visitors are not always welcome, particularly at the all-inclusives. If the resorts allow nonregistered guests, a stiff cover charge (or even a condition that you eat dinner there) may be required.

The entertainment offered is mixed in quality and usually falls into three categories: reggae, calypso, or current rock which, after being retranslated by the island band and singer, still sounds like reggae and calypso.

The best entertainment on the north shore is in Negril at the fabulous Disco at Hedonism II, the Tree House, and Club Kohuua. All offer live reggae. In Ocho Rios, try the Little Pub on Main Street in Ocho Rios, and in Montego Bay, visit Sir Winston's Reggae Club.

Don't, however, go out of your way to visit any of these clubs. If they are close, go; none are worth driving a long distance.

For more information contact the Jamaican Tourist Board at 866 Second Ave., New York, NY 10017 or call 212/688-7650. In Jamaica, the tourist board is in the Tourism Central Building, New Kingston, Box 360, Kingston Sides (809/929-9200). Tourist board offices are also at the two major airports.

PUERTO RICO

Puerto Rico, the fourth largest island in the Caribbean, has it all. Inviting beaches, a verdant and rugged countryside crowned by a national forest, exciting nightlife that is the envy of its neighbors, grand resorts, all forms of sports, and a deep Spanish tradition that is celebrated in its festivals and remembered in its numerous centuries-old buildings.

Puerto Rico's Spanish heritage can be traced back to 1493, when Columbus landed on the 1110-mile-long and 35-mile wide island, and 1503, when Juan Ponce de León established an outpost where Old San Juan is today.

Old San Juan, located on a leg-shaped spit of land flanked by the Bahia de San Juan and the Atlantic, awed us with its magnificent old buildings, some dating back to the sixteenth century. Before you take a tour of the historic area, pick up maps at tourism offices at 301 Calle San Justo (809/721-2400), in the old district.

The historic buildings include such sites as San Felipe del Morro, a massive (140 feet tall) fortress built by the Spaniards between 1540 and 1783; La Casa de los Contrafuertes, one of the oldest houses on the island; the sixteenth-century San José Church; the Dominican Convent built in 1523; Casa Blanca, the sixteenth-century masonry house that replaced the frame home of Ponce de León; and the San Juan Cathedral, built in 1540 and expanded over the centuries since.

Elsewhere in Old San Juan are graceful plazas, many craft shops and boutiques, museums of art and history, and colorful boulevards like the esplanade at the port, where strollers find an avenue filled with flowers, shade trees, and artisans hawking their creations. The best shopping in the old area is found on San Francisco, Fortaleza, and Cristo streets.

Crafts in Puerto Rico are superb. Visit the Institute of Puerto Rican Culture, in an ancient Dominican convent in Old San Juan, for exhibits and sales. Some of the best craft buys are the colorful paper mâché masks worn in annual festivals (buy them at Crafts,

Olé, Puerto Rican Art, or the Institute), the delicate lace called *mundillo* (buy it at Aquadilla en San Juan), or nineteenth-century *santos*, wooden statues of saints (Galería Botello).

New San Juan is no less an attraction. The Santurce district is known for its shops and markets, while Isla Verde is the place for sunbathing during the day and playing all night in the many casinos, nightclubs, and discos. The atmosphere at the casinos and clubs is exciting, but not necessarily romantic.

Outside the city are the natural attractions—beaches, a rain forest, small villages, and mountains. The best way to visit them is by rental car; but if you go, make sure you have a good map. Many of the country roads are unmarked.

One of your destinations may be the hundreds of beaches on the island. We found the best to be Luquillo Beach, 30 miles east of San Juan, and Isla Verde, the strand near the resort hotels just outside the city. On the south coast, try Punta Guilarte, near Arroyo, and Rosada, near La Parguera. On the north shore, the best beaches are Cerro Gordo, 25 miles west of San Juan, and Punta Salinas, near Dorado. The beaches on the west coast are not very good.

Near the Luquillo Beach is the 28,000-acre El Yunque rain forest. El Yunque, a variation of the Indian spirit Yuquiyu, is a lush wilderness filled with orchids, towering trees, vines, and ferns. The forest trails can be difficult; dress for the visit (hiking clothes and shoes) and go with a guided tour, which can be arranged at your hotel.

Fajardo, a large fishing and boating port on the eastern end of the island, is also the place you catch the ferry (fares are about $2–$2.50) to the offshore islands of Culebra and Vieques. On Vieques, try Sun Bay, and on Culebra, there are many small, white-sand beaches.

Another fascinating stop, near Utuado on the other end of the island, is the Caguana Indian Ceremonial Park, a centuries-old playground and religious site used by the Taino tribes. There you can see monoliths, petroglyphs, and a small museum.

Northwest of Utuado, on Route 129, is the Rio Camuy Cave Park, where guides will take you through some magnificent caverns and to an underwater river.

In the small towns and villages in the countryside, the Spanish heritage runs deep. The square in the center of the small town is where you will find the shops, restaurants, and historic sites. There is one slight drawback to exploring these towns on your own; unlike San Juan, English is not spoken as widely in the small villages, where the Spanish language, customs, and festivals are a way of life. That, we believe, is a major part of the charm of Puerto Rico.

If the beaches, lush forests, and mountain views are not romantic enough, visit the tiny fishing port of La Parguera on Phosphorescent Bay on the southeast coast of Puerto Rico. At night, the calm bay offers an unusual attraction, one we found both eerie and magical. Marine plankton in the water glows when disturbed by boats or any movement. Tour boats leave nightly at 7:30 from the La Parguera waterfront to give visitors a closer look at the phenomenon.

For us, moonlight on a bay is romantic. A bay that glows without any moonlight is just as moving.

Romantic Retreats

Some of the grandest and largest resorts in the Caribbean are found in Puerto Rico. These grand resorts are found in and around San Juan. For a quiet and less expensive alternative, try the small country inns called *paradores.* The *paradores'* rates range from $30 to $80 for a room for two. For reservations call 800/443-0266 or 809/721-2884 in Puerto Rico.

The rates are for a room for two per night and do not include meals unless noted. The three categories:

Inexpensive—Less than $100
Expensive—$100 to $200
Very expensive—$200 and more

Meal plans are offered at many hotels and can help cut costs. All-inclusive plans offer all meals, snacks, drinks, wine, entertainment, activities, sports, gratuities, and airport transfers for one fee, which ranges from $1,000 to $3,000 per person per week. Whether that is a bargain depends on how much you eat, drink, and play and whether you want more freedom to sample restaurants elsewhere on the island. Check your travel agent for current tariffs and the all-inclusive and other meal plans.

Our favorites in San Juan:

El San Juan Hotel and Casino. This large (393 rooms, 22 acres) resort on the Isla Verde beach offers modern and spacious rooms, tennis courts, water sports, nightclubs, and a casino. It's very lively, and that may be its only drawback. To add an air of romance, book the suites with sunken baths, spas, or gardens. Very expensive. 809/791-1000 or 800/468-2818.

Condado Beach Hotel. For style and old-fashioned elegance, it's hard to beat the Condado. Cornelius Vanderbilt built it in 1919, and today the 245-room hotel retains an old world charm. The pink lobby, flowers, Victorian furnishings in the common areas, and Spanish colonial items in the rooms combine to make this a special place. Facilities include a pool and water sports center. Expensive. 809/721-6090 or 800/468-2775.

Ramada Gran Hotel el Convento. This beautiful pink stucco building in Old San Juan was a Carmelite convent in the seventeenth century. Today, it offers 94 rooms (14 with balconies), a pool, and beach transport. It's very romantic, but we think it was nicer before they covered the inner courtyard with a sunroof. Expensive. 809/723-9020 or 800/468-2779.

Elsewhere on the island:

Horned Dorset Primavera Hotel. Face it. How many chances will you get to stay in a fantastic hotel named after a breed of English sheep? This hotel, in Rincón on the western coast, offers 26 beautifully furnished suites (four-poster beds, marble, French doors, patios) in three Mediterranean-style villas. Facilities include a pool, a water sports center at Club Náutico de Rincón. They sell a very peaceful and serene setting. Very expensive. 809/823-4030.

Hyatt Dorado Beach. Set on two lovely half-moon beaches, this resort in Dorado west of San Juan offers 1,000 acres of beautifully landscaped grounds, 300 spacious and comfortably furnished rooms, a casino, two golf courses, seven tennis courts, carriage rides, horseback riding, two pools, and more. Even with all these activities, a couple can find tranquility here. Very expensive. 809/796-1234 or 800/228-9000.

Hyatt Regency Cerromar Beach. Another Dorado resort, this Hyatt has a fantastic beach that is overshadowed by the man-made river pool, the longest freshwater pool perhaps in the world. It has an underground jacuzzi, 14 waterfalls, flumes, grottoes, and a current to slowly float you along to all these sights. The 504 rooms in the seven-story modern hotel are spacious and comfortably furnished. Facilities include casino, nightclub, 14 tennis courts, two golf courses, horses, and more. Very expensive. 809/796-1234 or 800/228-9000.

Palmas del Mar. This 2700-acre east coast resort set on a former sugar plantation offers accommodations in villas and apartments, three miles of beaches, 20 tennis courts, miles of hiking trails, golf, horseback riding, water sports, and occasional live entertainment. Very expensive. 800/221-4874.

Parador Banons de Coamo. This mountain inn north of Ponce is located near some hot sulphur springs that local legend sellers insist were Ponce de León's Fountain of Youth. Whatever, the 48 rooms are very comfortable. Expensive. 809/825-2186.

Parador Hacienda Gripinas. There are 19 attractive rooms decorated with crafts in this mountain hideaway near Jayuya. Inexpensive. 809/721-2400.

Parador Oasis. This two-century-old mansion near the town of San Germán in the western mountains has 50 rooms, but all the nice ones are in the front of the great house. The other rooms in an annex in back are like those in any other motel. Stick to the rooms in front or go elsewhere. Inexpensive. 809/892-1175.

On Vieques:

La Casa del Frances. This 12-room inn is, well, interesting. The atmosphere is that of a non-stop houseparty, the decor ranges from comfortable to rummage sale. It's minutes from a nice beach, and Room 12 is said to have a ghost. Still, it all adds up to a wonderful stopover, ghost or not. Inexpensive. 809/741-3751.

For information about homes you can rent in Puerto Rico, please read Chapter 10, "A Villa of Your Own."

Dining and Nightlife

Puerto Rico has many fine restaurants serving French, Spanish, Italian, and other familiar cuisines. But don't overlook island dishes, which usually include lots of fresh vegetables and all meats and fish rubbed with a marinade made of garlic and oregano.

The following price categories for restaurants are for dinner for two, without wine or alcoholic beverages:

Inexpensive—$30 and less
Moderate—$30 to $50
Expensive—$50 to $100
Very expensive—More than $100

In Old San Juan:

Amadeus. Its nouvelle Caribbean cuisine features some very creative seafood dishes. Moderate. 809/722-8635.

La Chaumiere. A fine country French fare is offered in an intimate setting. Very expensive. 809/722-3330.

Santiago. Here you are offered a beautiful setting with nouvelle

Caribbean cuisine. Stick to the fresh fish dishes. Very expensive. 809/723-5369.

In New San Juan:

La Compostela. Superb Spanish food favored by knowledgeable locals. Stick to seafood and lamb. Very expensive. 809/724-6088.

La Reina de España. The light green dining room's beauty is overshadowed by the beautiful and creative Castillian dishes. Very expensive. 809/721-9049.

Il Giardino. This rooftop restaurant in the Dutch Inn offers some stunning Italian creations and a red rose for every lady. Expensive. 809/722-1822.

Elsewhere on the island:

El Batey de Tonita. This mountain restaurant in Cayey serves such local favorites as guinea hen fricassee and rabbit. Moderate. 809/745-6312.

Gonzalez Seafood. Perhaps the finest seafood on the island is served here, in Cabo Rojos on the west coast. Moderate. 809/851-9000.

The Horned Dorset Primavera. Luxurious tropical setting and wonderful food accentuate this dining spot. Stick with the fish. Expensive. 809/823-4030.

For nightlife, try the casinos and the nightclubs in the big hotels. The best casinos are in the Sands Hotel, the El San Juan, the Hyatt Dorado Beach, and the Hyatt Regency Cerromar. For nightclubs, the Sands' Club Calypso books big-name acts like Jay Leno. El San Juan's Tropico favors revues and the Condado Plaza Hotel's La Fiesta offers sensual Latin shows and occasionally puts on flamenco and water ballet extravaganzas.

The hotels are also the sites of the year-long LeLoLai Festival, celebrating the island's Spanish, Indian, and African heritages in dance, music, and drama. There are shows every week, but the venue changes from hotel to hotel. Check with your concierge for the schedule and tickets.

Que Pasa?, the free guide available at tourism offices and at many other locations, lists current entertainment news.

For more information contact the Puerto Rico Tourism Company at 575 5th Ave., 23rd Floor, New York, NY 10017 or call 212/599-6292 or 800/ 223-6530. In Puerto Rico, call the tourism company at 809/721-2400. Their offices are at the Luis Munoz International Airport, or at 301 Calle San Justo and La Casita next to Pier One in Old San Juan. Elsewhere, the offices are located in city halls in the smaller towns.

Planter's Punch

Rum Punch or Planter's Punch is a popular drink in the islands, but exactly what goes into these red concoctions other than rum differs from island to island, from bar to bar. Despite the variations, the ingredients in this recipe make up the standard punch:

One measure of lime juice
Two measures of sugar syrup
Three measures of rum
Four measures of juices (choose what is fresh and available)
Five drops of bitters.
Add a dash of nutmeg spice, if you wish.
Serve over crushed ice.

The Saman Terrace at the elegant Carambolo Beach Resort and Golf Club on St. Croix.

CHAPTER 2

The Leeward Islands

THE MOST DIVERSE in the Caribbean, the Leeward islands offer visitors the flavor of their French, Dutch, British, American, and Danish cultures in settings that range from tiny quiet hideaways to livelier destinations with elegant resorts and electric nightlife.

The Leewards include the bustling U.S. Virgin Islands and St. Thomas, the shopping mecca of the region. "America's Paradise" is sharply different from the nearby British Virgin Islands, where the resorts are smaller and the pace more serene. If the British islands are not quiet enough, head to Anguilla, Nevis, or St. Eustatius, unspoiled islands offering some fine small inns and resorts and a lot of peace. St. Kitts is almost as quiet, but it does have one small casino and a few nightclubs.

Beach lovers and divers may find Antigua (365 beaches) and Barbuda (numerous shipwrecks and a superb reef) to their liking.

The influence of the Netherlands in the region lives on today in St. Maarten, which shares an island with the French St. Martin, and St. Eustatius.

For a taste of France with a West Indies accent, visit Guadeloupe, St. Martin, or St. Barthélemy, better known as St. Barts.

As for the British, the Empire may be broken up, but the British influence continues on Antigua, St. Kitts, Nevis, Anguilla, and the British Virgin Islands. (The British Crown Colony of Montserrat is not included in this guide because of the extremely heavy damage suffered during Hurricane Hugo in September 1989.)

Most of these islands are quite small (less than a hundred square miles) and you will find few golf courses, huge sports resorts, or large nightclubs. You will, however, find peaceful shores, a taste of a different but somehow familiar culture, and some very romantic inns and resorts.

ANGUILLA

Named by Columbus in 1493, the Anguilla (the Spanish word for eel), is a long narrow island that offers visitors little to do but enjoy the excellent beaches and serenity of an unspoiled land.

Considered by many visitors to be one of the Caribbean's best-kept secrets, Anguilla makes up what it lacks in lush vegetation, historic sites, shopping bazaars, and flashy nightlife with a peaceful atmosphere where visitors can actually get away from all the bustle and glitter of home.

Anguilla's main attractions are its 30 superb white-sand beaches and enough reefs to satisfy the diving and snorkeling set. We found the best beaches on Shoal Bay, on the western tip, and Cove Bay, Maunday's Bay, and Rendezvous Bay on the southern shore. For diving and snorkeling, the best reefs can be found at Mimi Bay, on the northeast shore, and around Sandy Island two miles offshore. Sandy is reachable by the ferry boat *Shauna* from Sandy Ground.

The center of civilization on the island is in the center in The Valley, which has one historic building, a few shops and restaurants, and little else worth seeing. The historic house is Wallblake House on Cross Roads. It was built around 1787 and is worth touring. The best part of a visit is listening to the legends of murder and corruption that are part of the house.

There are some shops in The Valley and elsewhere on the island, but Anguilla isn't a place for shoppers. No, the attractions on Anguilla are on the coast, where the rhythm of the waves can wash away the stress of life on the mainland.

Romantic Retreats

Small though it may be, Anguilla offers a wide variety of resorts and inns.

The rates are for a room for two per night, and do not include meals unless noted. The three categories:

Inexpensive—Less than $100
Expensive—$100 to $200
Very expensive—$200 and more

Meal plans are offered at many hotels and can help cut costs. All-inclusive plans offer all meals, snacks, drinks, wine, entertainment, activities, sports, gratuities, and airport transfers for one fee, which ranges from $1,000 to $3,000 per person per week. Whether this is a bargain depends on how much you eat, drink, and play and whether you want more freedom to sample restaurants elsewhere on the island. Check your travel agent for current tariffs and the all-inclusive and other meal plans.

Our favorites:

Cap Juluca. This Moorish-style resort offers 18 rooms in five villas set on 180 acres with a lovely beach. The rooms are luxuriously furnished, with solariums, marble baths, and private gardens adding to the attraction. This resort is expanding, so ask for a room away from the construction. Other facilities include tennis courts and water sports center. Very expensive. 809/497-6666 or 800/235-5305.

Cinnamon Reef Beach Club. The split-level villas at this 18-room resort offer modern furnishings, tropical decor, and beachfront locations. Facilities include pool, tennis courts, and a water sports center. Very expensive. 809/497-2727 or 800/223-1108.

Coccoloba Plantation. The 51 rooms in the oceanfront villas in this absolutely lovely resort have beautiful and colorful furnishings and such amenities as large marble baths (some with jacuzzis) and complimentary stocked refrigerators and minibars. There are also tennis courts, two pools, a sauna, exercise rooms, and water sports center. Very expensive. 809/497-6871 or 800/351-5656 (800/468-0023 in Canada).

Mallіouhana. The 52 rooms in this luxury hotel atop a bluff overlooking a secluded beach and cove are stunning! King-size canopied or platform beds, colorful Haitian-print decor, and marble baths make the spacious rooms and suites a very special retreat. Facilities include tennis courts, exercise room, and water sports center. Very expensive. 809/497-6111 or 212/696-1323.

The Mariners. This beachfront resort has 27 rooms in 18 West Indian–style guesthouses with verandas and lush vegetation. The Sandy Ground resort is very casual and the only attractions other than the beach are watersports and entertainment a few nights each week. Expensive. 809/497-2901 or 800/223-0079.

For information about homes you can rent, please read Chapter 10, "A Villa of Your Own."

On Location

What do James Bond, Superman, Dr. Doolittle, and Dustin Hoffman have in common?

They all made movies with scenes shot in the Caribbean.

Among our favorite movies made, all or in part, in the Caribbean are:

- *"Dr. No," shot in 1962 in Jamaica and "Thunderball," 1965 in Nassau. Both films starred Sean Connery.*
- *"Superman," shot in 1978 for the scene where the caped hero zooms to St. Lucia to pick up a bird-of-paradise blossom for Lois Lane. Christopher Reeves starred.*
- *"Dr. Doolittle," shot in 1967 on beautiful and lush Marigot Bay on St. Lucia. Rex Harrison starred.*
- *"Papillon," shot in Jamaica in 1973, with stars Dustin Hoffman and Steve McQueen.*
- *"Cocktail," some scenes shot in 1988 in Jamaica. Tom Cruise starred.*
- *"Clara's Heart," shot in Jamaica in 1988. Whoopi Goldberg starred.*
- *"The Deep," shot in the waters off the British Virgin Islands where the wreck of the R.M.S. Rhone off Salt Island was used in the movie. Nick Nolte and Jacqueline Bisset starred.*

Restaurants and Nightlife

The best restaurants are in the best resorts—the Cinnamon Reef Beach Club (Continental/Anguillian), Coccoloba Plantation (Continental), and Malliouhana (French). All are very good and expensive. You should call for reservations.

The following price categories for restaurants are for dinner for two, without wine or alcoholic beverages:

Inexpensive—$30 and less
Moderate—$30 to $50
Expensive—$50 to $100
Very expensive—More than $100

Our favorites elsewhere:

Hibernia. This lovely little (six tables) French restaurant in Sandy Ground serves superb grilled lobster and chicken dishes in a courtyard filled with flowers. Moderate. 809/497-3180.

Johnno's. Not so much a restaurant as a happening on Sunday afternoons in Sandy Ground when the band AngVibes makes the place rock while the patrons feast on barbecued fish, lobster, and chicken. Try it then and even when the band isn't playing. Moderate. 809/497-2728.

Lucy's Harbour View Restaurant. This terrace restaurant overlooking the sea in South Hill serves some fantastic seafood dishes, including Lucy's famed whole red snapper. Try the Creole and curried dishes, too. Moderate. 809/497-6253.

For nightlife, the Mayoumba Folkloric Group presents a comical song-and-dance revue at the Cul de Sac Inn's restaurant every Thursday night (809/497-6461). For music nightly, head to Cinnamon Reef and Cap Juluca.

For more information contact the Anguilla Tourist Information Office, c/o Medhurst & Associates, 271 Main St., Northport, NY 11768 or call 212/869-0402 or 800/553-4939. On Anguilla, the tourist office is in the Secretariat in The Valley (809/497-2759).

ANTIGUA

From the slopes of 1,330-foot-high Boggy Peak, the beauty of Antigua unfolds below: gentle green hills stretch down to seemingly endless beaches; blue-water harbors, alive with hundreds of yachts; and small towns vibrating with activity and history.

Antigua is an island that seems to have it all. The local tourism officials claim there are 365 beaches "one for every day of the year and every angle imaginable for optimal tanning." That may be hyperbole, but Antigua does have perhaps the Caribbean's largest collection of fine beaches, spread around the many isolated coves on the 108-square-mile island.

Although they were part of the lure for Richard Burton, Princess Margaret, and Madonna, who had their honeymoons here, the beaches are not the only attraction. The island's deep sense of its British history, coupled with a marvelous restored port, make this island one of the most attractive and interesting in the Caribbean.

There are two major cities on the island. St. John's, the capital on the northwest coast, offers a lively public market where island goods and crafts are sold and numerous shops and boutiques. Also worth visiting in St. John's is the Museum of Antigua and Barbuda (Antigua's sister island 30 miles north); St. John's Cathedral, built in 1681 and rebuilt after a nineteenth-century earthquake; and Redcliffe Quay, a popular area of restaurants, shops, and other markets on the site where slaves were once sold.

Shopping is a major attraction in St. John's, with the usual buys in perfumes, liqueurs, jewelry, and china. Don't miss the fine craft shops in Redcliffe Quay (the Pottery Shops and Things Antiguan) or Nelson's Dockyard (the CoCo Shop and Serendipity).

On the south coast is English Harbour, the port considered by many to be the most beautiful in the Caribbean; and Nelson's Dockyard, perhaps the island's most famous attraction. The Dockyard, commissioned in 1755, was the headquarters for Admiral Horatio Nelson when he was sailing the Caribbean to defend British interests.

The old buildings, ruins, and other landmarks of the Dockyard have been reborn, thanks to an active campaign by island citizens. Today, Nelson's Dockyard is a reborn historic area, filled with shops, restaurants, and bars. Nelson isn't forgotten; his telescope and tea caddy are among the many nautical artifacts in the Admiral's House Museum.

Other historic sights include the Master Shipwright's House, the Saw Pit, the old Officer's Quarters (now an arts and crafts gallery and workshop), the stately Copper and Lumber Store (now an inn), the ruins of Fort Berkely, and the fortifications on Shirley Heights. These last two attractions also have the best view of the spectacular harbor.

Elsewhere on Antigua we found Fig Tree Drive, 4 1/2 miles north of Liberta, to be a fascinating drive into the hills and the island rain forest. Figs you will not find, however; for Antiguans call bananas figs.

Another intriguing sight is near Jennings, where a small road will take you to the giant stone megaliths of Greencastle Hill. There are numerous theories of why the stones were put into place, but many researchers believe that they were used for religious or astronomical purposes. No one really knows.

On the eastern coast, near Willoughby Bay, is Harmony Hall, a sister of the famed art gallery near Ocho Rios in Jamaica. This gallery, located in an elegant stone building, displays and sells excellent paintings, crafts, and other works of art.

Beach lovers will need a map and a car to explore the many fine shores on the island. The most romantic are the white-gold sands of Morris Bay and the snow-white sands of Carlisle Bay, both on the southwest coast; the pink sands of Half Moon Bay on the southeast coast; and Long Bay, on the eastern coast, which also has a great snorkeling reef. Others that we enjoyed include Dickenson Bay on the northeast coast and Freeman's Bay near the entrance to English Harbour.

Thirty miles north is Antigua's sister island of Barbuda, a 12 by

5 mile spit of land reachable by daily LIAT flights or via Carib Link Ferry. Beaches surround Barbuda, and the best is Cocoa Point, a fine, eight-mile-long stretch of sand.

The main attractions at Barbuda are the numerous shipwrecks off the south coast, making this a treasure ground for divers. The Maartello Tower and Fort on the island were once used to report ship sightings and wrecks.

Also worth visiting on Barbuda is the island's bird sanctuary. Getting there is time-consuming, a 45-minute trip made in small boats, but the Frigate birds and the mangrove swamps make the trip worth the effort.

Romantic Retreats

Antigua offers a wide variety of resorts and inns, scattered all around the island. What doesn't vary so much is the cost; most places are very expensive. For cheaper accommodations, try the inns in Nelson's Dockyard.

The rates are for a room for two per night and do not include meals unless noted. The three categories:

Inexpensive—Less than $100
Expensive—$100 to $200
Very expensive—$200 and more

Meal plans are offered at many hotels and can help cut costs. All-inclusive plans offer all meals, snacks, drinks, wine, entertainment, activities, sports, gratuities, and airport transfers for one fee, which ranges from $1,000 to $3,000 per person per week. Whether that is a bargain depends on how much you eat, drink, and play and whether you want more freedom to sample restaurants elsewhere on the island. Check your travel agent for current tariffs and the all-inclusive and other meal plans.

Our favorites:

Admiral's Inn. This 14-room inn offers simple rooms in the colorful restored district of the Nelson's Dockyard. Inexpensive. 809/463-1027 or 800/223-5695.

Blue Waters Beach Hotel. The 67 rooms in the two- and three-bedroom beachfront villas are comfortable and attractive. Facilities include a tennis court, pool, and water sports center. Very expensive. 809/562-0290 or 800/372-1323.

Copper and Lumber Store Hotel. This wonderful inn is located in the former supply store for Nelson's Dockyard. The 14 suites are furnished with period antiques and four-poster canopy beds. Four of the suites are original to the building and are the best rooms. Expensive. 809/634-1058.

Curtain Bluff. This luxurious hotel, located on a peninsula bluff overlooking the Atlantic and Caribbean, is the center of many island social activities. And so it should be. The location overlooking the seas and two beaches is absolutely stunning. The 60 rooms are luxurious and spacious. Other facilities include tennis courts, croquet green, and water sports center. Very expensive. 809/463-1115.

Hawksbill Beach Hotel. Four beaches come with this fine resort, made up of 75 rooms in a great house and in cottages along the shore. The rooms are comfortable and furnished with wicker and gaily colored fabrics. Other facilities include a pool, tennis courts, and water sports center. Very expensive. 809/462-0301 or 800/327-6511.

Jumby Bay. On a 350-acre private island, this marvelous resort offers 38 suites in cottages and an atmosphere of casual elegance. Facilities include tennis courts and water sports center. Very expensive, but rates include all meals, drinks, and activities. 809/462-6000 or 800/437-0049.

St. James Club. A sister of the famed London establishment, this 105-room beachfront hotel offers elegant rooms, with canopy beds in the suites and villas. White Rolls-Royce buggies carry guests around the resort. Facilities include a dive school, casino, nightclub, croquet court, two pools, tennis courts, riding stables, and water sports center. Very expensive. 809/463-1430 or 800/274-0008.

Sibony Beach Club. Another beachfront beauty, this inn offers 12 suites, each with a private balcony or patio, beautiful furnishings, and small kitchen. Expensive. 809/462-0806 or 800/533-0234.

For information about homes you can rent, please read Chapter 10, "A Villa of Your Own."

Restaurants and Nightlife

Dining in this very British island tends to be more formal than on other shores. Call for reservations and ask about the dress code.

The following price categories for restaurants are for dinner for two, without wine or alcoholic beverages:

Inexpensive—$30 and less
Moderate—$30 to $50
Expensive—$50 to $100
Very expensive—More than $100

Our favorites, outside of the big hotels listed above:

Admiral's Inn. This 200-year-old inn in Nelson's Dockyard serves up some fine lobster and beef. Expensive. 809/463-1027.

L'Aventure. The terrace of this Divi Bay Resort restaurant in Long Bay has a sensational view, wonderful nouvelle Caribbean cuisine for lunch, and haute French cuisine for dinner. Expensive. 809/463-2003.

Clouds. The setting is stunning and the menu is creative at this restaurant overlooking Halcyon Cove. Dine on the terrace and feast on some of the finest food on the island. Try the noisettes of lamb and the breast of chicken. Expensive. 809/462-0256.

The Dolphin. This small restaurant near St. John's serves up some fine local dishes. Try the pepperpot and the fish. Inexpensive. 809/462-1183.

For nightlife, an afternoon barbecue with music at the Shirley Heights Lookout (809/463-1785) usually continues well into the night. The Chips disco at the Halcyon Cove Resort is a popular nightspot.

There are casinos in the Halcyon Cove Resort, the Flamingo, and the Royal Antiguan. The casino in the St. James Club is for guests only.

For more information write the Antigua and Barbuda Tourist Office at 610 5th Ave., Suite 311, New York, NY 10020 or call 212/541-4117. On the island, the tourist offices are at Long and Thames streets in St. John's (809/462-0480).

BRITISH VIRGIN ISLANDS

Picture this: a broad blue-green channel cutting a path between more than 50 islands ranging in size from almost unnoticeable up to two islands barely more than a dozen miles long. On these islands are small resorts and inns (nothing more than two stories high) and small harbor towns catering to passing sailors and other explorers.

On the shores of these islands are countless beaches, most of which are rarely visited. Around these islands are some of the finest sailing waters and anchorages in the Caribbean, scores of shipwrecks, superb diving, and fine fishing.

Though there are more than three score islands in and around the Sir Francis Drake Channel, there are only six that have resorts and attractions that we consider romantic.

The largest of the British Virgin Islands (BVI) is Tortola, only 15 miles long by 4 miles at its widest with a population of only about 9,000. Tortola is a quiet island; there is no city, even though there is a capital, Road Town. The capital is a popular port community, with hundreds of yachts making their home there and another 500 or so visiting every month.

The harbor is the center of life in Road Town, with ship stores, shops, and restaurants lining the harborfront. The shops near the water sell very expensive, very trendy items, but you might do better at the shops at your resort.

Elsewhere on the island, we found some stunning empty beaches and rugged mountains. The best beaches are Cane Garden Bay, on the north coast, whose eastern end is said to be popular with surfers during the winter, and Long Bay, on Beef Island (reachable by bridge from East End).

In the mountains just south of Cane Garden Bay is Sage Mountain National Park, the highest mountain (1,716 feet) in the Virgin Islands. The summit is covered by a lush rain forest, offering views of mahogany trees, elephant-ear vines, numerous birds, and stunning views of the Drake Channel.

The other large island in the BVI is Virgin Gorda, an odd-shaped island whose northern end is mountainous with a summit of 1,370 feet, and whose southern half is flat and covered with mammoth boulders.

Virgin Gorda is another favored destination of sailors, and the yacht harbor is the center of commerce on the island. Spanish Town, also called The Valley, is in the flat center of the island, but it is more a residential community for the island's 1,000 citizens than it is a commercial hub.

There are about a score of fine beaches on Virgin Gorda, and the most romantic is one whose main attraction is not the sand, but the giant boulders that line its shore and waters. On the southern tip of the island are The Baths, a popular spot for snorkeling, picnicking, sunbathing, and anchorage. At The Baths, enormous boulders lodged in the water and on the shore create grottoes, tiny coves, and underwater wonderlands.

In the sea, the boulders create a water wonderland of marine life, where we found colorful fish and strange coral of all sizes. The views were truly remarkable. (If you do go snorkeling, be aware of the strong shifting currents.)

The path down from the parking lot at the south end of the island is a steep narrow passage that may test the unfit. Once there, visitors will find other paths leading into seemingly impassable crevices between the boulders. Once through, you will find cathedral-like settings with shallow lagoons lit by small sunbeams. The sight is remarkable and beautiful.

At the other end of the island, from a wooden observation deck at the summit of Virgin Gorda Peak, the beauty of the Caribbean comes alive in unspoiled green islands and a sea of deep blues and many shades of diluted greens. In those waters are scores of shipwrecks, including the R.M.S. Rhone, a 310-foot-long steamer that went down in shallow water in 1867. The Rhone was used in the movie "The Deep."

Other islands in the BVI worth visiting are Peter Island, Guana

Island, and Marina Cay. All are known for secluded beaches, quiet, great snorkeling and diving, and wonderful resorts.

If you visit any of these islands, take time at night to find a quiet place to look out at the Sir Francis Drake Channel. At night, when the stars are out, this historic passage is empty of any signs of civilization. On the distant shores you will see no lights, no buildings, no signs of life; nothing but wonderful, peaceful, unspoiled islands.

Romantic Retreats

There are few rooms in the British Virgin Islands, fewer even than are in one single major hotel in San Juan. This means high prices and early reservations.

The rates are for a room for two per night and do not include meals unless noted. The three categories:

Inexpensive—Less than $100
Expensive—$100 to $200
Very expensive—$200 and more

Meal plans are offered at many hotels and can help cut costs. All-inclusive plans offer all meals, snacks, drinks, wine, entertainment, activities, sports, gratuities, and airport transfers for one fee, which ranges from $1,000 to $3,000 per person per week. Whether that is a bargain depends on how much you eat, drink, and play and whether you want more freedom to sample restaurants elsewhere on the island. Check your travel agent for current tariffs and the all-inclusive and other meal plans.

Our favorites on Tortola:

Fort Recovery. The nine villas surrounding a seventeenth-century fort are peaceful colorful retreats offering flower-filled patios and gardens, tasteful decor, and complete kitchens. The villas are on a small beach seven miles from Road Town. Rentals are usually for a week. Expensive. 809/495-4354.

Long Bay Beach Resort. Located on a marvelous, mile-long beach, this 52-room resort offers beautiful accommodations in cabanas and hillside complexes. Facilities include a pool, 9-hole pitch-and-putt golf course, and tennis courts. Expensive. 809/495-4396.

Prospect Reef. If water sports are your interest, this 131-room resort offers a harbor, lagoon, three pools, pitch-and-putt golf course, tennis courts, and water sports center. The rooms are spacious and have great views of the water. Expensive. 809/494-3311 or 800/356-8937.

Sugar Mill Hotel. The 20 rooms in this hillside inn are beautifully furnished. Facilities include a pool and a superb restaurant. Expensive. 809/495-4355.

On Virgin Gorda:

Biras Creek. Reachable only by boat, this elegant North Sound resort offers 32 deluxe suites, no roads, a garden and bird sanctuary, a pool, tennis courts, and beach. Very expensive. 809/494-3556.

Bitter End Yacht Club. The 100 rooms in this exquisite North Sound marina/resort are in luxurious villas on the beach and on the hill, or even at the marina on a luxury yacht. Facilities include a pool, numerous boats, and water sports center. Very expensive. 809/494-2746.

Little Dix Bay. One of our favorites in the Caribbean, this 102-room resort offers luxurious hexagonal-shaped rooms just steps away from a crescent beach and 400 beautifully landscaped acres. Facilities include tennis courts and water sports center. Expensive. 809/495-5555.

Olde Yard Inn. Famed for its extensive library, this 12-room inn is a short walk from a beach and an idyllic refuge offering simple but attractive guestrooms, a pleasant lounge for games and conversation, and a popular restaurant. Expensive. 809/495-5544.

On Peter Island:

Peter Island Hotel and Yacht Club. Elegant isn't the word for this complete resort offering beautifully furnished modern rooms, a pool, tennis, and horseback riding. The marina may be the best in the BVI. Very expensive. 809/494-2561.

On Guana Island:

Guana Island Club. There are 15 beautiful rooms at this luxury island hideaway. Very expensive. 800/54-GUANA.

On Marina Cay:

Marina Cay Hotel. There are 12 colorful and comfortable rooms in this hotel that is popular with sailors. Very expensive. 809/494-2174.

Romantic moments in the islands linger forever in the mind to be retrieved, savored, and enjoyed again and again. One of those moments for us came on the island of Virgin Gorda, during a stay at the wonderful Little Dix Bay resort.

There, after a fine dinner in the open-air pavilion, we listened to the music and danced to a few songs as we sat on the terrace overlooking the bay. Mostly, though, we gazed at the sky which glowed with stars.

After a while, we left the terrace and walked along the beach. By then the moon had risen; the sea, sand, and palm fronds glistened with a fine silvery light.

It was beautiful and very unforgettable.

Dining and Nightlife

With two exceptions, the big resorts listed above also offer the finest dining on the British Virgin Islands. All the resort menus feature seafood and expensive prices.

The following price categories for restaurants are for dinner for two, without wine or alcoholic beverages:

Inexpensive—$30 and less
Moderate—$30 to $50
Expensive—$50 to $100
Very expensive—More than $100

On Tortola, try these two restaurants:

Mrs. Scatliffe's Restaurant. This West Indian restaurant in Carrot Bay near the Sugar Mill offers some surprisingly good fish and more exotic items like chicken in a nut with herbs. Inexpensive/moderate. No phone.

Sugar Mill Restaurant. The owners of this restaurant and inn are known not only for the quality of the food in their intimate dining room, but also for the cookbooks (*Two Cooks in One Kitchen* and *The Sugar Mill Hotel Cookbook*) they have written. Try the West Indian lamb curry and grilled quail with papaya. Expensive. 809/495-4355.

For nightlife, in Tortola try Pusser's Landing (809/495-4554) on the West End or The Pub at the Fort Burt Marina (809/494-2608). Both feature live music.

In general, the entertainment at the resorts is good, and the ride to other nightspots usually isn't worth it.

For more information contact the British Virgin Islands Tourist Board at 370 Lexington Ave., Suite 511, New York, NY 10017 or call 212/696-0400. In the islands, the tourist offices are in Road Town near the ferry dock (809/494-3134). The free publication *The Welcome Tourist Guide*, given away at hotels and at other public places, is a useful guide to restaurants, sites, and other attractions.

GUADELOUPE

Guadeloupe is a French island, home to beautiful and rugged scenery, magnificent waterfalls, an active volcano, and perhaps the finest restaurants in the Caribbean.

The butterfly-shaped Guadeloupe is actually two islands—the 218-square-mile Grande-Terre and the 312-square-mile Basse-Terre, connected by a drawbridge over the sea channel dividing the two. Grande-Terre is where the best beaches and resorts are found, while Basse-Terre has a rugged coastline, numerous mountains, and wonderful scenery.

The 74,000-acre Basse-Terre Parc Naturel is a favorite of nature lovers, offering hiking trails, rivers, waterfalls, and tropical forests.

In the park is the volcano, La Soufriére. It's officially dormant, but has been emitting steam and sulphurous fumes from its vents and mud holes in recent years. The tourist office's *Guide to the Natural Park* outlines several hiking trails that will take you to the edge of the crater.

Other attractions on Basse-Terre include Les Chutes du Carbet, the three waterfalls on the southeast coast that caught Columbus' eye in 1493, and Trois-Riviéres, a seaside village whose small park has boulders bearing ancient Indian inscriptions.

Pigeon Island, just off Malendure Beach on Basse-Terre's western shore, has been acclaimed as one of the top diving places in the world. The Nautilus Club on the beach conducts scuba trips to the reefs there.

On Grande-Terre, the attractions are more urbane. Ste. Anne, St.-François, and Le Moule are small villages with colorful buildings and wonderful beaches.

Caravelle Beach near Ste. Anne has reefs that make it a good place for snorkeling. Raisins-Clairs, popular with windsurfers, and Tarare, popular with nudists, are near St.-François on the southern shore.

The major city on Guadeloupe is Pointe-á-Pitre, a city of 100,000 known for its colorful and busy Marketplace at rues Frébault, Schoelcher, Thiers and Peynier, and its superb duty-free district nearby.

Pointe-á-Pitre has a few historical buildings, but the busy streets, noise, and constant traffic make it an unpleasant place to visit. Don't go if you are not going there to shop.

The best buys are the usual luxury items (expect a discount of around 20 percent) and rum. Crafts range from the shoddy to the sensational. The Au Caraibe at 4 rue Frébault and Tim Tim at 16 rue Henry VI have some wonderful crafts and antique items.

Gosier, on the southern coast of Grande-Terre, is the center of the major resorts, and has numerous shops, discos, and restaurants.

Finally, one of the best reasons for coming to Guadeloupe is the food. Mix the cuisine of France with the cultures of Africa, India, South America, and other nationalities and you have a culinary feast.

The island's residents know just how important food is to their lives. The island's more than 100 restaurants are one indication. The second is the Fête des Cuisiniéres (Festival of Chefs), which takes place every August and honors St. Laurent, patron saint of chefs, with a parade of cuisiniéres to the Cathédral de St. Pierre et St. Paul. There, a mass is celebrated and is followed by an afternoon of music, food, and dance.

(Traveler's note: French is the language of the island, and outside of the big hotels and inns, visitors will find few English speakers [or at least few who will admit it]. A small knowledge of French and perhaps a small English-French dictionary will help make your trip more pleasant.)

Romantic Retreats

If the big resorts are not your cup of tea, try a Relais Creole, the French-style inns which have been approved by the tourist office.

The rates are for a room for two per night and do not include meals unless noted. The three categories:

Inexpensive—Less than $100
Expensive—$100 to $250
Very expensive—$250 and more

Meal plans are offered at many hotels and can help cut costs. All-inclusive plans offer all meals, snacks, drinks, wine, entertainment, activities, sports, gratuities, and airport transfers for one fee, which ranges from $1,000 to $3,000 per person per week. Whether that is a bargain depends on how much you eat, drink, and play and whether you want more freedom to sample restaurants elsewhere on the island. Check your travel agent for current tariffs and the all-inclusive and other meal plans.

For romantic atmosphere, our recommendations are:

Auberge de la Distillerie. Close to the Parc Naturel, this seven-room country inn also offers a rustic chalet that can sleep up to four. The rooms are fine, but you may have to share a bath. Inexpensive. 590/94-25-91.

Auberge de la Vielle Tour. The 80 rooms in this fine 1950s-style hotel are comfortable, but the real attractions of this resort are the dining room, the beach, the numerous water sports, and the nightly entertainment. Other attractions include a pool, tennis, nearby golf, and boat trips. Expensive. 590/84-23-23.

Cap Sud Caraibes. This Relais Creole inn offers 12 comfortable rooms in an equally comfortable and welcoming atmosphere. Expensive. 590/88-96-02.

Grand Anse Hotel. This Relais Creole hotel has 20 bungalows, spectacular mountain views, a black sand beach about a mile away, and a lush setting near Trois Riviéres. Inexpensive. 590/92-92-21.

Hamak. One of the more beautiful resorts on the island, the 57 suites in the bungalows are on a stunning crescent beach, surrounded by more than 10,000 trees and flowers. Each bungalow has its own walled garden, giving guests a maximum of beauty and privacy. Other attractions include water sports, boat excursions, tennis, and a Robert Trent Jones golf course. (Guests are guaranteed tee times.) Very expensive. 590/88-59-99.

Relais du Moulin. The 20 rooms in this inn on a former sugar plantation are located in the bungalows behind the old sugar mill.

The suites in the bungalows are small and simply furnished, but the location in the peaceful lush countryside near Chateaubrun is worth a visit. Expensive. 590/88-23-96.

La Toubana. The 57 rooms in the hillside bungalows overlooking the Caravelle Beach are comfortable but simply furnished. Facilities include tennis courts, a pool, and a water sports center. Expensive. 590/88-25-78 or 800/223-9815.

On the Iles des Saintes (12 miles south of Basse-Terre):

Auberge des Anacardies. The 10 rooms in this popular inn and restaurant in Terre-de-Haut are comfortably furnished and have breathtaking views of the gardens and bay. Inexpensive. 590/99-50-99.

For information about homes you can rent, please read Chapter 10, "A Villa of Your Own."

Dining and Nightlife

Dining is so wonderful on this island that the only problems you will have are selecting from the many fine restaurants and then dieting to take the pounds off. The chief cuisine is Creole, although classic French is very popular. Popular Creole dishes include spicy fish stews, curried meats, and cod fritters (called *accras*), all accompanied by native vegetables and fruits. Jackets and reservations are required at many restaurants; call ahead.

The following price categories for restaurants are for dinner for two, without wine or alcoholic beverages:

Inexpensive—$30 and less
Moderate—$30 to $50
Expensive—$50 to $100
Very expensive—More than $100

Our favorites (but there are so many, many others worthy of mention):

Auberge de St.-François. This elegant country home in St.-François specializes in crayfish but also serves many other fine fish dishes. Dinner is served either in the intimate dining room or outside on the patio surrounded by flowers. Expensive. 590/88-51-71.

Auberge de la Vielle Tour. This fashionable restaurant in Gosier is famed for its French cuisine, with a touch of the tropics. Expensive. 590/84-23-23.

La Balata. Classic Lyon cuisine is accented with Creole flair in this popular Gosier restaurant. The best tables are on the terrace, where the view is wonderful. Expensive. 590/90-88-25.

Le Barbaroc. There are only 12 tables at this very creative Creole restaurant in Petit Canal. Don't miss the "punch de maison." Inexpensive. 590/22-62-71.

La Canne á Sucre. This restored colonial house in the center of Pointe-á-Pitre serves some of the best and most creative dishes on the island. Expensive. 590/82-10-19.

Chez Clara. This popular Creole restaurant in Ste. Rose is often crowded, but the food is worth it. Moderate. 590/28-72-99.

Chez Violetta-La Creole. The chef in this Gosier dining spot is Violette Chaville, head of the association of cuisiniéres, who serves some of the best Creole dishes on the island. The waitresses are dressed in Caribbean costume. Inexpensive. 590/84-10-34.

Relais du Moulin. Grouper and lobster are the house specialties in this nouvelle restaurant in Chateaubrun. Expensive. 590/88-13-78.

For nightlife, the most popular discos are Le Caraibe in Gosier (590/84-22-22) and the very French Elysée Matignon in Bas-du-Fort (590/90-89-00). Most of the major resorts have nightclubs with live entertainment on most nights.

There are two casinos on the island: The Casino de Gosier les

Bains in Gosier (590/84-18-33) and the Casino de St.-François in St.-François (590/84-41-40).

For more information contact the French West Indies Tourist Office at 610 5th Ave., New York, NY 10020 or call 212/757-1125. The tourist offices on the island are at 23 rue Delgrés in Pointe-á-Pitre (590/82-09-30), in Maison du Port in Basse-Terre (590/81-24-83), and on the Ave. de l'Europe in St.-François (590/88-48-74).

ST. BARTHÉLEMEY

Small, casual but very chic, the French island of St. Barthélemey (St. Barts) is an unspoiled paradise with beautiful beaches, elegant homes, superb food, and a picturesque harbor.

The beaches on St. Barts are similar to the beaches on the French Riviera. Topless bathing is common, but nudity is not. Our favorite beaches are the Petit Anse de Galet near Gustavia and Colombier on the northeast coast, where a 30-minute hike from La Petit Anse will take you to a very private stretch of sand. Other popular spots include St. Jean, with its nearby cafés, and Anse du Gouverneur, which has a great view of St. Kitts and St. Eustatia.

In the small harbor town of Gustavia, the corner cafes, small luxury shops, and excellent restaurants would fit into any stylish Côte d'Azur resort in France. The shops in the village can be found on rues Roi Oscar II and du Général de Gaulle.

A drive around the 8-square-mile island takes you to many interesting villages, scenic overlooks, and fine beaches, but few noteworthy historical sights. During the drive you might see women wearing starched bonnets similar to those worn in Brittany. That's because the islanders are descendants of Normans and Bretons, as well as Swedes.

Romantic Retreats

The rates are for a room for two per night, and do not include meals unless noted. The three categories:

Inexpensive—Less than $100
Expensive—$100 to $200
Very expensive—$200 and more

Meal plans are offered at many hotels and can help cut costs. All-inclusive plans offer all meals, snacks, drinks, wine, entertainment, activities, sports, gratuities, and airport transfers for one fee, which ranges from $1,000 to $3,000 per person per week. Whether that is a bargain depends on how much you eat, drink, and play and whether you want more freedom to sample restaurants elsewhere on the island. Check your travel agent for current tariffs and the all-inclusive and other meal plans.

Our favorite romantic places on the island:

Castelets. The antique-filled rooms in this Provençal-style inn are beautiful, but cannot match the stunning views from the hilltop location. There are 10 rooms; a few are in the main house and the rest in villas. All are luxuriously decorated. Facilities include a small pool and a beach reachable by car. Very expensive. 590/27-61-73.

Filao Beach Hotel. This elegant beachfront resort offers 30 spacious and beautifully furnished rooms. Unfortunately, only four have a view of the lovely water; the other 26 face the garden. Amenities include a pool and water sports. Expensive. 590/27-64-84.

François Plantation. The 12 pavilions in this French colonial plantation are furnished in simple, but stylish tropical decor: rattan furniture and mahagony four-poster beds. The views from some of the pavilions and the hilltop pool are stunning. Facilities include a pool. Very expensive. 590/27-61-26.

Hotel Guanahani. The largest resort on the island, this 76-room hotel offers luxurious rooms in cottages decorated with gingerbread trim. The cottages are on the beach or on the hillside, all with breathtaking views. Facilities include suites with private pools, a full spa, tennis courts, a pool, and water sports center. Very expensive. 590/27-66-60.

Hotel Manapany. The 52 rooms in this hotel on the Anse des Cayes cove come in hillside cottages or in beachfront suites with four-poster beds. The suites are much larger and nicer. Facilities include a pool, tennis court, and water sports center. Very expensive. 590/27-66-55.

El Sereno Beach Hotel. The 20 rooms in the quiet elegant retreat surround a garden, just steps from the beach. The rooms are small, but nicely furnished. Amenities include a pool and water sports. Expensive. 590/27-64-80.

For information about homes you can rent, please read Chapter 10, "A Villa of Your Own."

Dining and Nightlife

The cuisine and the prices on this island are first-class. Take advantage of the fixed-price menus and always make reservations. Then enjoy!

The following price categories for restaurants are for dinner for two, without wine or alcoholic beverages:

Inexpensive—$30 and less
Moderate—$30 to $50
Expensive—$50 to $100
Very expensive—More than $100

Our favorites:

Castelets. The hilltop setting and the classic French cuisine are difficult to match for romance. Very expensive. 590/27-61-73.

Gloriette. This casual beachside restaurant serves some superb local seafood. Moderate. 590/27-75-66.

La Crémailllére. This 200-year-old country house in Gustavia is a chic dining spot serving fine seafood. The house lobster special and lobster thermidor are super. Very expensive. 590/27-63-89.

François Plantation. The dining room at this colonial plantation features classic French cuisine in an attractive setting. Expensive. 590/27-78-82.

L'Hibiscus. The location overlooking the harbor and the nightly jazz performance makes you overlook any shortcomings in the food. Expensive. 590/27-64-82.

Le Marine. Fresh seafood (including mussels from France) and omelets make this dockside spot a great bargain. Inexpensive. 590/27-64-50.

Le Relais. Dine on the porch and enjoy some fantastic curried and Creole seafood. Moderate. 590/27-73-00.

Le Toque Lyonnaise. Another candidate for the best restaurant on the island, this open-air restaurant at the El Serene Beach Hotel in Grand Cul-de-Sac serves classic dishes from Lyon. Expensive. 590/27-64-80.

Restaurant Ballahou. Perhaps the most elegant restaurant on St. Barts is the pink-and-white dining room in this Anse des Cayes house, next to the pool. Mix in music, candlelight, and a fine menu featuring lobster, duck, and pigeon and you have almost all you need for a romantic meal. Very expensive. 590/27-66-55.

For nightlife, try the jazz lounge in L'Hibiscus or the Autour du Rocher (590/27-60-73), a disco and billiard room. The most popular nightspot in Gustavia is Le Select, where celebrities and those who wish to see them gather for a drink and talk.

For more information contact the French West Indies Tourist Board at 610 5th Ave., New York, NY 10020 or call 212/757-1125. On the island, the tourist offices are in the Mairie de St. Barth, rue August Nyman, Gustavia (590/27-60-08).

ST. EUSTATIUS

The tiny Dutch island of St. Eustatius is a quiet retreat, one whose handful of resorts and restaurants is overshadowed by its natural wonders.

St. Eustatius, more commonly called Statia (pronounced Stay-sha), is only eight square miles in size. Within those few acres is the Quill, an extinct volcano whose cone soars almost 2,000 feet. Inside the dormant crater is a rain forest, filled with majestic trees, wild-flowers, birds, orchids, fruit trees, and countless varieties of plants. There are a number of hiking trails leading to the crater, and the tourist office can help you hire a guide to lead you.

The best beaches on this tiny island are Smoke Alley Beach, with black and beige sands on the western coast, and Corre Corre Bay on the Atlantic side. The Atlantic surf is rougher.

In the clear waters offshore, underwater sights include numerous shipwrecks and submerged seaports.

The clifftop capital, Oranjestad, was built in 1736 when Fort Oranje was built by the Dutch. The town is home to numerous eigh-teenth-century buildings, including the Statia Museum in Upper Town, which displays numerous historic artifacts from the precolonial pe-riod. Nearby are the ruins of the Dutch Reform Church and Honen Dalim, the second synagogue in the western hemisphere. In Lower Town, below the fort's walls, you can stroll through the ruins of the eighteenth-century commercial center of the island. Outside of town is Sugarloaf, a cone-shaped mountain offering stunning views of St. Kitts and the seas.

There is little shopping and almost no nightlife (by one count there are only three bands on the island). But for a couple seeking an active yet quiet vacation, Statia may be the place.

Romantic Retreats

There is really only one very romantic inn on the island and that's the Old Gin House in Oranjestad. There are 20 rooms in this renovated eighteenth-century cotton gin and warehouse. The balconies are covered with colorful bougainvillaea, and the view below is of the pool and courtyard. The rooms are very comfortable and are furnished with antiques. The rates are expensive (more than $100 per night). 599/3-2319.

For information about homes you can rent, please read Chapter 10, "A Villa of Your Own."

Dining and Nightlife

St. Eustatius is not known for an abundance of fine restaurants, either. Actually, there just aren't many on the island. Call for reservations.

The following price categories for restaurants are for dinner for two, without wine or alcoholic beverages:

Inexpensive—$30 and less
Moderate—$30 to $50
Expensive—$50 to $100
Very expensive—More than $100

Our choices:

La Maison sur Plage. This French restaurant in Zeelandia serves a wonderful duck breast and entrecote. Expensive. 599/3-2256.

Mooshay Bay Public House. This restaurant in the Old Gin House (see above) serves a fixed-price, four-course dinner that includes some stunning dishes. Favorites are the snapper or the roast duck. Two wines come with the meal. Expensive. 599/3-2319.

Old Gin House. Eat on the terrace at this old hotel and enjoy some island seafood dishes or just a simple sandwich. Moderate. 599/3-2319.

L'Etoile. West Indian specialties and more familiar sandwiches are served at this Oranjestad spot. Inexpensive. 599/3-2299.

Stone Oven Bar & Restaurant. This cozy little house in Upper Town offers some fine West Indian and local dishes, served either in the gaily decorated rooms or outside in the garden patio. Moderate. 599/3-2247.

Nightlife is, in a word, limited. The island's three bands take turns at various spots in town. Ask around to see who has them tonight.

For more information contact the St. Eustatius Tourist Information Office, c/o Medhurst & Associates, 271 Main St., Northport, NY 11768 or call 512/261-7474 or 800/344-4606. On the island, the tourist office is at the entrance to Fort Oranje (599/3-2433).

ST. KITTS AND NEVIS

Separated by a two-mile wide strait, the guitar-shaped St. Kitts and the oval Nevis form a two-island nation known for its abundant natural wonders, lush vegetation, uncrowded beaches, and quiet resorts.

St. Kitts, at 65-square miles (almost twice the size of the Nevis), was known as St. Christopher until 1988 when it officially changed names.

Most of the attractions of St. Kitts are all near the coast, for the center of the "guitar's" body is bisected by a rugged mountain range, topped by the 3,792-foot peak of Mt. Liamuiga, a long dormant volcano. In those mountains are beautiful waterfalls and lush forest. Though there are trails into these mountains, it is not recommended that visitors go without a guide. Kriss Tours (809/465-4042) leads treks to the Mt. Liamuiga crater and to other mountain attractions.

The beaches are all on the southern end of the island, and some of the best are reachable only by boat. Try Banana Bay, Frigate Bay, and White House Bay. Elsewhere, two black sand beaches are popular with water sports enthusiasts: Conaree Bay on the east coast is favored by surfers, while Dieppe Bay on the north shore draws snorkelers and windsurfers.

The main town on St. Kitts is Basseterre, where the tourist offices can give you maps to the island and city. Basseterre is worth a walking tour; its graceful buildings and peaceful streets are very inviting.

Duty-free devotees will find the shops on Shoreline Plaza on the waterfront limited in number, but not so limited in bargains. On Bay Road are two shops selling some fine works of art. The Spencer Cameron Art Gallery sells a wide range of artwork, including the watercolors of British painter Rosey Cameron-Smith. Craftshouse offers crafts of wood, copper, and other island materials.

Other attractions in Basseterre include the Bay Street Market, which is a bustling bazaar on weekends when the islanders sell their produce. St. George's Anglican Church on Cayon Street was built in

1670 by the French who first called it Notre Dame. After numerous fires, quakes, and storms, it was rebuilt and renamed in 1859 by the British. Independence Square, on Bank Street, is a lovely garden, a peaceful site that makes one forget that slaves were once sold on the spot.

On the island's west coast, Brimstone Hill is the major attraction. The 38-acre stone fortress, once called the Gibraltar of the Caribbean, offers spectacular views from its cannon-studded ramparts. Built in 1736, the fortress was the scene of several spectacular battles between the British and French. A museum on the site displays artifacts and other historical items.

Two miles by ferry boat across the Narrow Straits, the 36-square-mile island of Nevis (pronounced Neevis) has a history almost as rich. John Smith stopped here in 1607 on his way to found Jamestown; Admiral Lord Nelson was married to a local lass here; and Alexander Hamilton, secretary of the Treasury under George Washington, was born here.

The island is filled with natural beauty and wonders. It has a half-dozen mineral baths whose reputed curative powers made the island a spa popular with Europeans in the seventeenth and eighteenth centuries.

The interior of the island, like St. Kitts, is crowned by a volcanic mountain range. Nevis Peak, its top 3,232 feet high, is almost in the center of the island, and often is hidden in clouds.

Charlestown is the capital of Nevis, with about 1,200 of the island's 9,000 residents. It's a pleasant town, but one with few attractions. The Alexander Hamilton birthplace on the waterfront is a beautiful seventeenth-century Georgian home that also holds the Museum of Nevis History and the Nevis House of Assembly.

Shoppers in Nevis will be frustrated unless they like stamps or batik. The Philatelic Bureau opposite the tourist office sells some beautiful and costly items, and Caribelle Batik in the Arcade is known for its colorful accessories.

The best beaches on Nevis are Pinney's Beach, a beautiful strand on the west coast, and the black sands of Oualie Beach just north.

One site you should not miss during a visit is the ruins of the famous Bath Hotel, just south of Charlestown. This spa was built on some of the mineral springs in 1778 and attracted as many as 50 guests a day during the boom times. The hotel is in ruin today but the adjacent bath house and springs are open to visitors.

One other famous house on the island's east coast is known for its sad tale of violence, love, and ghostly presences. The Eden Brown Estate was built around 1740. In 1822, Julia Huggins, who lived at the estate, was to marry a local fellow named Maynard. Unfortunately, on the day of the wedding the best man and Maynard fought a duel. Both men were killed. Miss Huggins never recovered from the shock and was rarely seen afterward. Locals today swear they can feel her ghostly presence near the top of the old house.

Romantic Retreats

Most of the guestrooms on St. Kitts and Nevis are in small plantation houses, country inns, and small hotels.

The rates are for a room for two per night and do not include meals unless noted. The three categories:

Inexpensive—Less than $100
Expensive—$100 to $200
Very expensive—$200 and more

Meal plans are offered at many hotels and can help reduce costs. All-inclusive plans offer all meals, snacks, drinks, wine, entertainment, activities, sports, gratuities, and airport transfers for one fee, which ranges from $1,000 to $3,000 per person per week. Whether that is a bargain depends on how much you eat, drink, and play and whether you want more freedom to sample restaurants elsewhere on the island. Check your travel agent for current tariffs and the all-inclusive and other meal plans.

Our favorite places on St. Kitts:

The Golden Lemon. This seventeenth-century French manor house made of coral stone is legendary. The 18 rooms in this inn are exceptional, perhaps the finest and most interesting in the Caribbean. Each has a name (Hibiscus Room, Turtle Room, Batik Room) and its own distinctive decor. The Hibiscus has two white canopy beds, while the Batik has antique beds. The antique-filled manor is on a black-sand beach on a lagoon. A walled garden offers a serene retreat, while outside the estate a colorful fishing village may tempt you to take a walk. There are 16 other rooms available in antique-filled condominiums, but stick to the manor house if possible. Facilities include a pool and tennis courts. Very expensive. (Minimum four-day stay in season, maximum 14-day stay anytime.) 809/465-7260.

OTI Banana Bay Beach Hotel. Accessible only by boat, this 20-room inn on the peninsula between the Banana Bay and Cockleshell Bay beaches offers spacious rooms and lots of privacy. Facilities include a water sports center. Expensive. 809/465-2754 or 800/223-5695.

Rawlins Plantation. Surrounded by fields of sugarcane, this plantation offers 10 rooms in cottages around the great house. The tower of the seventeenth-century windmill is a duplex suite, while the other cottage rooms offer simple but attractive furnishings. Facilities include a pool, croquet, tennis, beach transportation, and boat cruises. Expensive. 617/367-8959.

Our favorites on Nevis:

Croney's Old Manor Estate. Located on the side of Mt. Nevis, this 10-room inn sits amid beautiful tropical gardens on a former sugar plantation. The rooms are large and attractively furnished with period reproductions. Facilities include a pool. Expensive. 809/465-5445 or 800/223-9815.

Golden Rock. There are 16 beautiful spacious rooms in the five cottages with verandas on this 200-year-old sugar plantation. Among the attractions here are the beautiful tropical gardens with orchids, restored buildings, and mountain location. The inn has cabanas on two beaches and provides shuttle bus transportation to them. Facilities include a pool, bike rentals, and water sports. Expensive. 809/469-5346 or 800/223-9815.

Montpelier Plantation Inn. There are 16 guest cottages surrounding the West Indian–style grey stone house on this 650-acre estate where Admiral Nelson married Fanny Nisbet in the eighteenth century. The rooms are large and pleasantly furnished. Amenities include transportation to the inn's cabana at Pinney's Beach, horseback riding, and water sports. Very expensive. 809/469-5462 or 800/243-9420.

Nisbet Plantation Inn. This two-story stone plantation great house is nestled in 40 acres of coconut palms, which make a beautiful setting for a sunset. The 31 rooms are in 17 gingerbread-trimmed cottages on the palm-shaded grounds just a short walk from the beach. The rooms are simple but comfortable. Amenities include tennis and water sports. Expensive. 809/469-5325.

For information about homes you can rent, please read Chapter 10, "A Villa of Your Own."

Dining and Nightlife

The following price categories for restaurants are for dinner for two, without wine or alcoholic beverages:

Inexpensive—$30 and less
Moderate—$30 to $50
Expensive—$50 to $100
Very expensive—More than $100

Our choices on St. Kitts:

Frigate Bay Beach Hotel. This is an exception to the usual rule about hotel dining rooms: The candle-lit setting overlooking the pool is romantic, and the curried and Creole seafood dishes are wonderful. The hotel is in Basseterre. Expensive. 809/465-8935.

The Georgian House. Antiques, candlelight, a magnificent old Basseterre manor house with a fine continental menu. Expensive. 809/465-4049.

The Golden Lemon. The beautiful dining room and flower-filled patio are the setting for exceptional meals featuring West Indian and continental dishes. Expensive. 809/465-7260.

The Patio. The flowers filling this Dieppe Bay house make this intimate dining spot very special. The six-course, fixed-price menu features seafood and is served by reservation only. Expensive. 809/465-8666.

Victor's Hideaway. This friendly casual restaurant behind the Church of the Immaculate Conception in Basseterre serves excellent curried dishes and fried seafood. Inexpensive. (They don't have a phone so you may want to stop by earlier to make a reservation or just wait. It's worth it.)

Our favorites on Nevis:

The Cooperage. This dining room in Croney's Old Manor Estate features local seafood and curried dishes served in a quiet colonial atmosphere. Expensive. 809/469-5445.

Hermitage. Stick with the West Indian specialties at this intimate, candle-lit restaurant in the Hermitage Plantation Inn in St. John's. Expensive. 809/469-5477.

Nisbet Plantation Inn. The antique-filled dining room features fine West Indian and continental dishes. Stick with the seafood. Expensive. 809/469-5325.

For nightlife on St. Kitts, A.J.'s Place (809/465-6264) across from Brimstone Hill is the local nightspot. The Royal St. Kitt's Casino (809/465-8651) in Jack Tar Village in Frigate Bay is a casual gambling spot. On Nevis, the hotels often have entertainment on weekend nights. Otherwise, try the Mariner's Pub & Bar (809/469-1993) near Fort Ashby. Local reggae and calypso bands play there.

For more information contact the St. Kitts & Nevis Tourist Board at 414 E. 75th St., New York, NY 10021 or call 212/535-1234. In St. Kitts, the tourist offices are on Church Street in Basseterre (809/465-4040 or 2620). In Nevis, the offices are on Main Street in Charlestown (809/469-5521, ext. 2049).

ST. MAARTEN/ST. MARTIN

Exquisite beaches, two distinctly different and charming cultures, great restaurants, a huge lagoon made for water sports, and enough nightlife to keep you up later than you want make the 37-square-mile island of St. Maarten/St. Martin a refuge for travelers seeking an island with a bit of everything.

St. Maarten (the Dutch side of the island) and St. Martin (the French side to the north) do have a few shortcomings. There are no lush rain forests, no slumbering volcanoes, no historic forts or cities filled with sixteenth-century buildings, and little cultural life.

The island is shaped like a triangle, with a massive hole (Simpson Bay Lagoon) near its western tip. The lagoon attracts almost as many boaters, windsurfers, and snorkelers as the numerous fine beaches. The two best stretches of sand are on the French side, on the island's western tip. Baie Longue is a mile-long stretch of empty shore, but the surf can be rough. Baie Rouge on the northwest shore is beautiful and is a clothing-optional shore. Cupecoy Beach, just south of Baie Longue on the Dutch side, is secluded and is made very scenic by its neighboring cliffs and caves.

The capital of the Dutch half of the island is Philipsburg, on the southern coast of the triangular-shaped island. Wathey Square is the center of town, home to the tourist office and the Town Hall, which is the white building with the cupola.

The streets and lanes (*steegjes*) off the square are lined with restaurants and duty-free shops. The latter are legendary in this part of the world. By one estimate, there are 500 duty-free shops in St. Maarten. Front Street, Old Town near the end of Front Street, and the new Amsterdam Shopping Center stock the usual luxury items, but we like the crafts and locally made gifts in the Shipwreck Shop and Sasha's.

Outside of Philipsburg, Front Street becomes Sucker Garden Road and leads into the mountains for some stunning views of the coast and sea.

On the French side of the island are several places worth a visit. North of Orleans on the northeast coast is the village of French Cul de Sac, a beautiful area with magnificent colonial great houses and great hiking trails.

St. Martin's two big cities are Grand Case and Marigot. Marigot is the capital, and is a haven for shoppers. Rues de la Liberté and de la République are the places to head with your credit cards.

Grand Case is where you head with your appetite. The main street of this small town has more than two dozen restaurants featuring fine French, Indonesian, Vietnamese, and other cuisines.

In short, the attractions of St. Maarten/St. Martin are simple—warm sun, soothing surf, gourmet food, and wonderful shops. What more can a couple ask?

Romantic Retreats

The rates are for a room for two per night and do not include meals unless noted. The three categories:

Inexpensive—Less than $100
Expensive—$100 to $300
Very expensive—$300 and more

Meal plans are offered at many hotels and can help cut costs. All-inclusive plans offer all meals, snacks, drinks, wine, entertainment, activities, sports, gratuities, and airport transfers for one fee, which ranges from $1,000 to $3,000 per person per week. Whether that is a bargain depends on how much you eat, drink, and play and whether you want more freedom to sample restaurants elsewhere on the island. Check your travel agent for current tariffs and the all-inclusive and other meal plans.

Our choices on St. Maarten:

Caravanseri. The 84 rooms in this lovely, art-filled hotel on a bluff above Maho Bay are spacious and furnished with individual decor. Some of the rooms have small private pools. Facilities include two pools, a shuttle to the casino, and water sports center at Mullet Bay Resort. Very expensive. 599/5-42510 or 800/223-9815.

Oyster Pond Yacht Club. This 20-room, partially round hotel on a bluff overlooking gardens and sea is an exquisite retreat. The rooms are large, furnished with colorful designer fabrics and prints and imported wicker. Facilities include a beautiful beach, gardens, stunning new pool, tennis courts, and water sports center. Very expensive. 599/5-22206.

Passangrahan Royal Guest House. Queen Wilhemina stayed in this stately old inn that was the governor's residence in the late 1800s and home to the Queen and Princess Juliana during World War II. There are 31 rooms in this Dutch colonial mansion in downtown Philipsburg, many with balconies and most with four-poster king-size beds. The most romantic is the Queen's Room, No. 21, reached by a staircase adorned with bougainvillaea. Expensive. 599/5-23588 or 800/622-7836.

On St. Martin:

La Samanna. This is one of the most beautiful and secluded resorts in the Caribbean. With white villas, flower-filled grounds it offers a great view from its hillside location. There are nine rooms and two suites in the luxurious main house located in a garden overlooking Baie Longue. The rooms are nice, much nicer than the 74 apartments and multi-bedroom villas nearby. Facilities include a pool and tennis courts. Very expensive. 590/87-51-22 or 212/696-1323.

La Belle Creole. One of the most romantic resorts we know, La Belle Creole is a fantasy, a Mediterranean village built around a central plaza. The 156 rooms and suites are large and furnished with every modern convenience. The resort is stunning, but doesn't have the charm found in non-chain resorts. Facilities include three beaches, a pool, and tennis courts. Very expensive. 590/87-58-66 or 800/HILTONS.

Hevea. This small but romantic inn has eight beautifully furnished rooms. Expensive. 690/87-56-85.

L'Habitation. The 250 kitchenette suites in this Neo-Victorian are lovely, adding to the attraction of a resort with a beautiful beach, pool, and superb restaurants. Very expensive. 590/83-33-33 or 800/847-4249.

For information about homes you can rent, please read Chapter 10, "A Villa of Your Own."

Dining and Nightlife

There are scores of fine restaurants on this island and it's difficult giving you just a few.

Prices are expensive on both sides of the island. Reservations are required at most places during the high season. (Note: To call a restaurant on the Dutch side from St. Martin, dial 3 plus the local number; to call a restaurant on the French half from St. Maarten, dial 06 plus the local number.)

The following price categories for restaurants are for dinner for two, without wine or alcoholic beverages:

Inexpensive—$30 and less
Moderate—$30 to $50
Expensive—$50 to $100
Very expensive—More than $100

Our favorites on St. Maarten:

Le Bec Fin. Famed for its lovely garden as well as its red snapper with mussel sauce, this Philipsburg restaurant is a beautiful place for a dinner. Very expensive. 599/5-22976.

Le Bilboquet. You have to make reservations a day in advance at this tiny hillside home in Pointe Blanche. The five-course, fixed-price menu is posted daily out front. Check it and then add your name to the reservation list if you want to dine the next evening. Very expensive. (No phone.)

L'Escargot. One of the island's oldest French restaurants, L'Escargot is located in a marvelous old house in Philipsburg and serves up some classic dishes accented by the island's own produce. Expensive. 599/5-22483.

Felix. You can enjoy candlelight dining alfresco next to the sea at Pelican Key, with creative French dishes. Expensive. 599/5-42797.

Oyster Pond Yacht Club. Elegant decor competes with the excellent seafood dishes at this restaurant in the hotel of the same name. Very expensive. 599/5-22206.

Spartaco. This 200-year-old house in Cole Bay serves superb seafood and pasta dishes as well as classic northern Italian cuisine. Very expensive. 599/5-45379.

Wajang Doll. Try the rijsttafel—the famed Indonesian rice feast—at this Philipsburg restaurant. Dine in the garden. Inexpensive. 599/5-22687.

On St. Martin:

L'Aventure. A beautiful restaurant with a bougainvillaea-filled veranda overlooking the Marigot harbor, and the French cuisine is just as fine. Very expensive. 590/87-72-89.

La Belle France. Located in the L'Habitation resort, this superb dining room features creative seafood dishes. Very expensive. 590/87-32-32.

Le Poisson d'Or. Fish is the featured entree at this elegant restaurant set in a restored stone house. Very expensive. 590/87-72-45.

La Provence. Very chic dining terrace at this restaurant set next to the plaza at La Belle Creole. Try the grilled lobster and the fresh pasta dishes. Very expensive. 590/87-58-66.

La Samanna. One of the most beautiful in the Caribbean, this restaurant serves superb Creole and French dishes. Try to dine on the terrace by candlelight, under the tent surrounded by tropical blooms. Baie Longue. Very expensive. 590/87-51-22.

La Residence. A fountain provides the background music at this romantic seafood restaurant in Marigot. Expensive. 590/87-70-37.

Nightlife in St. Martin consists mainly of dining and dancing. On St. Maarten, however, where there are eight casinos, things are much livelier. They are the Casino Royale at Maho Beach, the Great Bay Beach Hotel, Divi Little Bay Beach Hotel, Seaview Hotel, St. Maarten Beach Club, Pelican Resort, Mullet Bay Hotel, and Treasure Island at Cupecoy.

The top nightclubs are Le Club in Mullet Bay (599/5-42801), Studio 7 atop Casino Royale at Maho Beach (599/5-42115) and Night Fever in Colombier near Marigot (no phone). On St. Martin, the Le Privilege (9590/87-38-38) in Anse Marcel draws the chic set.

For the latest information on island nightlife, pick up the free publications entitled *Discover St. Martin/St. Maarten, St. Maarten Nights* or *St. Maarten Events.* These publications are distributed in the tourist information offices and at most hotels.

For more information contact the St. Maarten Tourist Office at 275 7th Ave., New York, NY 10001 or call 212/989-0000. For St. Martin, write the French West Indies Tourist Board at 610 5th Ave., New York, NY 10020 or call 212/757-1125.

On St. Maarten, the tourist information office is on Cyrus Wathey Square in Philipsburg (599/5-22337). On St. Martin, the tourist office is on Marigot Pier (590/87-53-26).

U.S. VIRGIN ISLANDS

"America's Paradise," the advertisements call the U.S. Virgin Islands. Surprisingly enough, the islands of St. Thomas, St. John, and St. Croix come close to living up to that slogan.

Where else can you find three islands so close together that meet all of your desires? St. Thomas is busy, booming, and a shopper's paradise. Three miles west, St. John is the serene garden spot of the three, home to undeveloped national parkland and unmatched beaches. Forty miles south lies St. Croix, the largest of the three islands and a blend of natural beauty, Danish heritage, and old stone mills.

We spent our honeymoon on two of these islands, St. Croix and St. Thomas. And while the islands have changed over the years (and not always for the better), they remain very special to us.

St. Thomas is the Virgin Island most visitors see. The main airport is there and the port at Charlotte Amalie, the busiest in the Caribbean, welcomes as many as 11 cruise ships at a time. The quaint narrow streets of the town are the Caribbean's shopping mecca. All this makes St. Thomas a very busy island.

Before exploring the island, stop at the Visitors Center on Tolbod Gade a few steps north of the waterfront and get maps of Charlotte Amalie and the island. The maze of streets, alleys, and island roads requires a map to sort out.

The main attractions in St. Thomas are in the busy streets that line the hillside between the Waterfront Highway and Main Street. On or between these two busy arteries are the numerous "alleys"—narrow, occasionally beautiful corridors lined with shops, restaurants, and tropical plants and trees. The main shopping district is bordered by Storetvaer Gade on the west and Tolbod Gade on the east, the two names are testimony to Denmark's ownership of the islands until 1917.

In this area of restored warehouses are scores of shops offering bargains on china, crystal, perfumes, clothing, liquor, and more. And if that isn't enough, the new Havensight Mall, at the cruise ship docks on the east end of the harbor, offers even more shops. As you can imagine, the two shopping districts can get quite crowded, particularly when there are many cruise ships in port.

If you enjoy seeing a little of the history of the island, you may want to tour Fort Christian, a striking rust-red castle at the Waterfront Highway. The fort was built in 1671 by the Danes and has served many governmental functions including housing prisoners. The cells now hold a small museum of Arawak and Carib Indian artifacts.

Up the hill from the fort, on Kongens Gade, is the surprisingly modest white-frame structure that is the Government House, the residence of the governor of the islands. Among the murals on the first two floors are works by Camille Pissarro, the father of French Impressionism. Just a few steps away is the Hotel 1829, a fine inn and restaurant and a lovely building erected in that year by a French sea captain.

Farther uphill, you will see the five-story stone tower that was built in 1679. The tower is part of Fort Skytsborg, a seventeenth-century fortress that is now the inn known as Blackbeard's Castle.

Downhill, on Crystal Gade, is the synagogue of St. Thomas' small Jewish community. This lovely structure was built in 1833 on the site of an earlier building, and the sand on the floor came from Israel and is a reminder of the Exodus.

There are more historical buildings, but nothing exceptional. What St. Thomas also offers in abundance are some striking beaches. The best beaches on this island (and on all of the Virgin Islands) are at the resorts listed below. All are open to the public, although that doesn't mean you can use the resort chairs or mats without paying a fee.

Off the beach, the other attractions on St. Thomas include Mountain Top, a lookout point 1,547 feet above the sea, where you can see as many as 18 islands on clear days; and Drake's Seat, which overlooks Magen's Bay. (Locals claim the bay is heart-shaped, but even romantics will have to stretch their imagination to agree.) The stone bench opposite the ever-present vendors is on the spot where Sir Francis Drake is said to have watched out for enemy vessels.

On Route 38 in the mountains is Jim Tillet's Art Gallery and

Boutique. Here artists create and sell their works of ceramics and silk-screened island prints.

Leave the mountains and head down to the lovely north coast, where you will find Coki Beach and the Coral World Marine Park. The beach is popular with snorkelers and the Marine Park has a number of exhibits displaying marine life. The newest exhibit is a house-size, round aquarium in which you view the fish from the center; in it a reef is recreated and populated by fish and other sea life. A short walk away over a bridge is the two-story viewing tower. The upper level contains shops while the lower level has windows allowing close-up views of fish, coral, lobster, and other sea inhabitants on the bottom of the cove. Other displays include pools with turtles and baby sharks, a parrot cage, and other sea life in numerous small aquariums.

A better view of reef life can be had on the *Atlantis*, a real submarine that operates from the cruise ship docks near the Havensight Mall. The sub holds 48 persons and takes one-hour day and night dives along a reef, reaching a depth of 90 feet. The night dives are said to be sensational, for the marine life displays its true colors under the bright floodlights of the submarine.

Continuing east along the north shore, you come to Red Hook Harbor, where you can catch the hourly ferry to St. John, which we believe is the most scenic and charming of the Virgin Islands.

The ferry docks in the harbor in Cruz Bay, one of the more interesting towns in the Caribbean because it has a number of artists' galleries and boutiques on the waterfront and along the streets back from the water. The open-air multilevel arcade called Mongoose Junction, on the north side of town, features some fine gift shops and a lovely restaurant.

Cruz Bay is small enough to take a leisurely walk around in about a half of a day. The only maps you will need from the National Park Service Visitors Center (located on the ferry dock) are those to the rest of the island and its hiking trails.

More than two-thirds of St. John is a national park, created in 1956 from land donated by Laurence Rockefeller whose family created the lavish Caneel Bay resort on the island. In addition, there are 5,600 acres of underwater national park for you to enjoy.

From Cruz Bay the North Shore road continues past some famous beaches. The first is Hawksnest, used in the movie "The Four Seasons," and then Trunk Bay, popular for its marked snorkeling trail.

On the north coast is the Annaberg Plantation, a major sugar producer in the eighteenth century. The plantation has been partially rebuilt. After the lush vegetation of the western half of the island, the eastern half may come as a surprise. It's drier, and many cactus plants can be seen growing around Coral Bay. The views here, like those from all the coastal roads, are spectacular.

Bordeaux Mountain is both a rain forest and, at 1,277 feet, St.

One morning as we were sunning ourselves on the beach outside our room at the Caneel Bay resort on St. John, a small dark object in the water kept catching our eye. By the time we raised our heads and looked at the water, the object had vanished.

At first, we dismissed this as a passing snorkeler or perhaps a floating coconut. But it happened so often that we finally put down our books and stared out at the sea, daring the object to reappear.

It did. Actually, they did. The dark objects were the heads of sea turtles, coming up for air.

We quickly put on our snorkeling masks and fins and swam out to where we last saw the turtle heads. There, through the clear water, we saw the two-foot-round turtles feeding calmly on plants on the sea floor. As they slowly began to swim up, we followed. Even though the turtles' movements were slow, they actually swam very fast, quickly leaving us behind as they surfaced for air and then headed out to deeper water.

For us, our moment with the turtles remains one of those crystal-clear memories of our visits to the islands.

John's highest point. Reef Bay Trail, a hiking route, will take you to the strange rock carvings that are attributed to Arawak Indians.

Forty miles south of St. John and St. Thomas is St. Croix. The 23-mile by 6-mile island suffered heavy damage from Hurricane Hugo in September 1989. The major resorts are expected to reopen in late 1990, and the small inns, shops, and restaurants in the cities of Christiansted and Frederiksted were also working hard to get things back to normal. Check with your travel agent before you plan your trip.

When St. Croix is able to welcome tourists again, they will find a lush island, filled with large old plantations and greathouses, a rain forest, and numerous empty beaches.

One sight not damaged by the storm was Buck Island's spectacular reef, an underwater national park. Snorkelers will love the reef and its colorful and active marine life, and nonswimmers can share the thrill by taking a glass-bottom boat tour to the island.

Before you leave the islands, take time to go to the Harbor View Inn on Frenchman's Hill in Charlotte Amalie. We spent three days of our honeymoon in this lovely, eighteenth-century French Huguenot villa. At night, on the open-air terrace overlooking the harbor, order a glass of wine and ask the pianist to play one of your favorites. On the water and land below you, the lights move endlessly, transforming the Virgin Islands into a real paradise.

Romantic Retreats

The Virgin Islands offer some fine resorts, inns, and condominium developments. Some of the best values may be on St. Croix, as it works to reattract tourists driven away by the aftermath of Hurricane Hugo.

The rates are for a room for two per night and do not include meals unless noted. The three categories:

Inexpensive—Less than $100
Expensive—$100 to $200
Very expensive—$200 and more

Meal plans are offered at many hotels and can help cut costs. All-inclusive plans offer all meals, snacks, drinks, wine, entertainment, activities, sports, gratuities, and airport transfers for one fee, which ranges from $1,000 to $3,000 per person per week. Whether that is a bargain depends on how much you eat, drink, and play and whether you want more freedom to sample restaurants elsewhere on the island. Check your travel agent for current tariffs and the all-inclusive and other meal plans.

Our favorites on St. Croix (the choices are limited at this writing; more resorts will reopen later):

The Buccaneer. We spent a week of our honeymoon in this lovely resort set on a hill overlooking the tennis courts, golf course, and beach. The 148 rooms in the lovely pink-stucco main house and adjacent villas are comfortable, offering balconies which overlook the water and the stone towers of old windmills. Other amenities include a health spa, horseback riding, golf course, and water sports center. Very expensive. 809/773/2100 or 800/223-1108.

Carambola Beach Resort and Golf Club. Until recently this was a Rockresort property offering 156 rooms and one suite in beautiful Mediterranean-style villas in a lush, garden-like location. Facilities include tennis courts, golf course, pool, and water sports center. Very expensive. 809/778-3800.

Cormorant Beach Club. The 38 rooms in the villas in this quiet, palm-shaded resort are spacious, colorful, and stylish. The best part of the club is the secluded beach and exciting reef a short swim away. Facilities include a pool, tennis courts, and water sports center. Very expensive. 809/778-8920.

On St. John:

Caneel Bay. This magnificently landscaped, 170-acre development has seven lovely beaches and 171 rooms furnished with stylish contemporary furnishings accented with lovely tropical fabrics. Caneel Bay is great for the couple that appreciates natural beauty and understated elegance. The only complaint we have is the abundant mosquito population, which doesn't respect elegance. This former Rockresort just changed owners and we understand they plan some changes. Stay tuned. Other facilities include a pool, tennis courts, and water sports center. Very expensive. 809/776-6111.

Virgin Grand Beach Hotel. This splashy 264-room, Art Deco-style resort just outside Cruz Bay has gorgeous suites and villas; the latter has huge marble whirlpool baths. The 34 acres of grounds are lush and carefully designed to be as striking and functional as any visitor could want. Facilities include a pool, tennis courts, and water sports center. Very expensive. 809/776-7171 or 800/323-7249.

Gallows Point. The 60 comfortable kitchenette apartments in this attractive complex on top of a waterfront bluff near Cruz Bay have striking views. Unfortunately, the beach is miniscule. Facilities include a pool. Expensive. 809/776-6434 or 800/323-7229.

On St. Thomas:

Elysian Resort. There are 66 spacious and beautifully furnished rooms in this elegant beachfront resort on Cowpet Bay next to the St. Thomas Yacht Club. The one-bedroom loft suites (the bedroom is in the loft, facing a second balcony) have striking views of the beach and pool. Facilities include tennis and water sports. Very expensive. 809/775-1000 or 800/223-1588.

Harbor View. This 10-room inn has been called "very Tennessee Williams" by *Harper's Bazaar*. It's true, but the real attractions of this inn are the antique-filled rooms, the pool-terrace overlooking Charlotte Amalie, and the serenity of the hillside location. Inexpensive. 809/774-2651.

Hotel 1829. The location isn't the best—on the eastern edge of the busy shopping district in Charlotte Amalie—but the 15 rooms in the rust-red, hacienda-style building have hosted dancer Mikhail Baryshnikov, King Carol of Romania, and Edna St. Vincent Millay.

Some of the rooms are tiny, so go for the more expensive rooms overlooking the pool and flower-filled courtyard. Expensive. 809/776-1829 or 800/524-2002.

Mark St. Thomas. The eight rooms in this 200-year-old funky inn have an unusual and colorful decor. It's a great little inn. Facilities include a tiny pool. Expensive. 809/774-5511 or 800/343-4085.

Pavilions & Pools. Each of the 25 rooms in this complex is attractive and comes with a full kitchen, but the main draw here is that you get your own pool and a feeling of complete privacy. The nearest beach is on the adjacent property. Expensive. 809/775-6110 or 800/524-2001.

Point Pleasant. The view of St. John and the Sir Francis Drake Channel is stunning at this 148-room hillside resort. The rooms range from simple to very elegant and spacious. Facilities include free use of a car for four hours a day, two beaches, three pools, tennis courts, and water sports center. Very expensive. 809/775-2000 or 800/524-2300.

Sapphire Beach. Located on one of the island's prettiest beaches, this 141-room resort offers spacious and modern accommodations, most of which have balconies and patios facing the seas. Amenities include tennis courts and water sports. Very expensive. 809/775-6100 or 800/524-2090.

Stouffer's Grand Beach Resort Hotel. This first-class resort may be the most complete on the island. The 290 rooms are attractive and spacious, each with balconies offering a view of the sea. Amenities include a small beach, two beautiful pools, tennis courts, and water sports. Very expensive. 809/775-1510 or 800/468-3571.

For information about homes you can rent, please read Chapter 10, "A Villa of Your Own."

Dining and Nightlife

The following price categories for restaurants are for dinner for two, without wine or alcoholic beverages:

Inexpensive—$30 and less
Moderate—$30 to $50
Expensive—$50 to $100
Very expensive—More than $100

Until St. Croix has fully recovered from the effects of the hurricane, we hesitate to recommend any restaurants beyond the resorts we mentioned. Christiansted, however, had numerous fine dining spots before the storm and will have them again. The best—pre-Hugo—were the Cormorant Beach Club (809/778-8920), Serendipity (809/773-5762), and the famed Club Comanche (809/773-2665).

On St. John:

Ellington's. Creative seafood dishes served in a casual setting at the Gallows Point resort outside Cruz Bay. Don't miss the Caribbean buffet on Sunday. Moderate. 809/776-7166.

Lucy's. This casual Cruz Bay spot is where Lucy Smith serves up some of the best native dishes on the island. Try the conch stew, piquant chicken, and fried plantain. Moderate. 809/776-6804.

The Sugar Mill Kitchen, the Beach Terrace Dining Room, and Turtle Bay Dining Room. These dining rooms at the Caneel Bay resort serve absolutely superb food, particularly on Wednesday night when the steak cookout is held. Reservations a must. Expensive. 809/776-6111.

On St. Thomas:

Agave Terrace. Mixing American nouvelle with Caribbean standards, this lovely dining room in the Point Pleasant resort is worth the trek to get to it. Expensive. 809/775-7200.

Gregerie East. The attraction of this restaurant is the view of the lovely boats passing by in the East Gregerie Channel. The menu features lamb chops and beef, but stick with the seafood. Moderate. 809/774-2252.

Harbor View. The hostess guides you to the open air terrace for a drink and time to study the menu. After you order, you wait on the terrace, admiring the view and the piano music. Only after your dinner is ready are you seated. Stick with the shrimp or beef. Expensive. 809/774-2651.

Hotel 1829. The seafood and steaks are wonderful, but don't miss the prize-winning soufflés. Expensive. 809/776-1829.

Victor's Hide Out. This hilltop restaurant is popular with celebrities and serves up fine seafood and ribs. Expensive. 809/776-9379.

Sightseeing Submarines

One of the hottest tickets in the islands today is for a sightseeing tour that takes place about 100 feet below the ocean's surface.

During a recent visit to St. Thomas we took a ride on the submarine Enterprise, *one of four shallow-diving sightseeing subs. (The other three sail from Grand Cayman, Barbados, and Bermuda.)*

The Enterprise *is 65 feet long and about 13 feet wide, the nautical version of a tour bus. We took a ferry from the cruise ship docks in Charlotte Amalie out to a nearby island, where we rendezvoused with the surfacing* Enterprise.

We and the other adventurers climbed down a steep staircase and entered the round body of the sub. There, a long row of back-to-back benches stretched down the center of the sub, allowing the passengers to sit and face the large viewing portholes on the sides.

After a few brief remarks to the 47 passengers, the three crewmembers started the engines and the submarine began to submerge into a world of ever-dimmer green.

The views were absolutely amazing. Even though we have snorkeled extensively and taken glass-bottom boat tours, nothing prepared us for the myriad forms of marine life and the endless configurations and colors of the coral reefs.

Identifying the passing fish was easy, for we were given cards showing pictures of the fish and naming them. We counted at least 12 species of fish during the dive.

We saw yellowtail snappers, stingrays, Caribbean parrot fish, angel fish, and other warm-water species. We also were surprised when we passed a female scuba diver, who was collecting shells. She held them up so we could see them.

The ride was unlike any other sightseeing tour we had taken. Better yet, the next time we go we plan to take the night dive, when the sub's floodlights bring out the brilliant colors of the fish and coral.

For nightlife on all the islands, check the major resorts. Most of them offer live entertainment most evenings, with a special calypso beach party once a week.

For more information write the U.S. Virgin Islands Government Tourist Office at 1270 Avenue of the Americas, New York, NY 10020 or call 212/582-4520. On St. Thomas, the tourist offices are at the airport, on Toldbod Gade near the waterfront, and in Havensight Mall. Call 809/774-8784. On St. Croix, the tourist offices are in the Old Scalehouse in Christiansted (809/773-0495). And last, but not least, on St. John the offices are on the ferry dock in Cruz Bay (809/776-6450).

The Hotel La Toc and La Toc Suites on St. Lucia, one of the most beautiful and dramatic resorts in the Caribbean. (*Photo courtesy of M. Silver Associates.*)

CHAPTER 3

The Windward Islands

THE SEVEN ISLAND GROUPS that make up the Windward Islands are among the most beautiful in the Caribbean.

Five of the islands—Dominica, Martinique, St. Lucia, Grenada, and St. Vincent—are legendary for their flower-filled rain forests, and extensive spice, fruit, and banana plantations that cover their majestic mountains and valleys.

The tiny Grenadines are less imposing geologically, but no less beautiful for they are sparsely developed and uncrowded, offering pristine beaches and crystal-like water. Barbados, the last of the Windwards, makes up for its lack of expansive rain forests with endless fields of sugar cane, miles of white-sand beaches, and historic old churches and great houses.

These islands have long been popular with Britons, Canadians, and Europeans; but Americans too have discovered that though the Windwards are a bit farther away, the wonders they hold are worth the journey.

BARBADOS

From the air, Barbados looks like the typical American countryside: a rolling landscape marked by small subdivisions and small farms whose green squares are neatly outlined by fences and roads.

The only Caribbean island that hasn't changed colonial masters, Barbados is a well-developed country with a stable government, well-educated populace, a sense of English culture, fine (by Caribbean standards) roads, an ever-present sugar cane industry, and enough scenic delights to entice any visitor.

Barbados is an oval island, 21 miles by 14 miles, made up of coral rock. Most of the land is rolling farmland with only a small mountainous region in the north-central part of the island.

The capital city is Bridgetown, a colorful and bustling city often described as a shopping mecca. It does have some shops on Broad Street, but the "mecca" part is overrated. The shops are neither numerous nor exceptional.

What is exceptional in Bridgetown is the Cheapside Market on Lower Broad Street which buzzes on Saturday mornings with vendors and buyers.

Cutting through the center of town is the Careenage, a fingerlike harbor that is home for pleasure yachts as well as fishing boats. The waterfront cafes across from Trafalger Square are excellent spots to sit and people-watch.

On the east side of town is Queen's Park and the Queen's Park House, the former home of the British commander that is now used as a theater and restaurant.

On the Caribbean coast north of Bridgetown is the spectacular Folkestone Underwater Park, where a marked underwater trail takes you over the sights of Dottin's Reef.

In the center of the island are several attractions. Harrison's Caves have golden caverns, underground lakes and waterfalls, and a small electric train to take you through them. The Flower Forest is a hillside garden offering spectacular vegetation and some stunning views of the rest of the island. In the clay mountains nearby are the Chalky Mount Potteries where the descendants of English potters have been making pots for three centuries.

A bit north, the Barbados Wildlife Preserve has exotic animals and birds, but no cages. You walk into the preserve with the animals. Just across the road is Farley Hill, the striking mountaintop ruin of a plantation great house. In the late 1950s, the plantation was restored and used in the movie "An Island in the Sun." Unfortunately, the restoration work was destroyed by fire several years later, but the ruins are a majestic sight to see.

On the north end of the island is the Animal Flower Cave, an oceanfront cavern that is home to delicate sea anemones.

Finally, there is the Atlantic Coast, perhaps the most striking coastal drive in the Carribean and one that rivals the Big Sur. On this rugged coast you will find huge waves driven by the trade winds, massive boulders larger than a house at water's edge, and rough clay and coral hills eroded and sculpted by wind and rain into striking shapes.

As tempting as the long empty beaches are, swimmers are not allowed except at a small beach in the village of Bathsheba. The waves, currents, and rocks are too deadly a combination. (The surfers you will see are usually locals who know the water and the rocks.)

All the beaches on the calmer Caribbean side are superb, varying only in width. The beach at Holetown near the Folkestone Marine Park is a popular strand although other swimmers swear by Browne's Beach in Bridgetown and Greaves End Beach south of the capital. The best beaches are at the hotels, and though they are often considered private, you can walk from one beach to another.

There are two cautions about the beaches. Vendors rove the beaches selling everything from jewelry to clothing. Most accept a simple "not-interested," but some are downright pushy. Report them to the hotel. Finally, on some of the beaches, jet ski vendors zoom around offering to take you for a ride. The ride is okay, but the jet skis do present a safety hazard when the drivers put selling ahead of keeping a safe distance from swimmers. The hotel beaches use floats and ropes to mark the swimming area and to prevent the jet skis from entering. This isn't always so on the beaches that aren't located at a hotel. Be careful.

Finally, Bajans (as the islanders are known) insist that the sunsets in Barbados are more colorful, redder, than the evening lightshows on other islands. This is so, say the researchers, because the skies are filled with very fine red sand from the Sahara that the trade winds have blown across the Atlantic. The sand also produces a haze which causes area sailors to complain because it creates a problem when sailing far offshore.

Knowing all that, we carefully watched to see whether the sunsets were redder or more dramatic thant the acclaimed sunsets at Negril in Jamaica.

The sunsets certainly were beautiful and colorful. But redder? We couldn't agree. You will have to make up your own minds.

Romantic Retreats

The rates are for a room for two per night and do not include meals unless noted. The three categories:

Inexpensive—Less than $100
Expensive—$100 to $200
Very expensive—$200 and more

Meal plans are offered at many hotels and can help cut costs. All-inclusive plans offer all meals, snacks, drinks, wine, entertainment, activities, sports, gratuities, and airport transfers for one fee ranging from $1,000 to $3,000 per person per week. Whether that is a bargain depends on how much you eat, drink, and play, and whether you want more freedom to sample restaurants elsewhere on the island. Check your travel agent for current tariffs and the all-inclusive and other meal plans.

Our selections:

Cobblers Cove Hotel. This 38-suite resort is very casual, unlike its guest list that has included such notables as Ronald Reagan. All the suites are large andd tastefully decorated. Facilities include a beach and pool. Very expensive. 809/422-2291.

Colony Club. The 76 rooms in this cottage colony are spacious and tastefully furnished, located on particularly lovely landscaped grounds. Facilities include a pool, beach, and water sports center. Very expensive. 809/422-2335.

Coral Reef Club. The grounds are lovely at this beachfront resort. There are 70 rooms in the cottages, and, while the decor once was very casual, the owners are slowly putting in less casual furnishings. Facilities include a pool. Very expensive. 809/422-2372 or 800/223-1108.

Crane Beach Hotel. This stunning hotel's swimming pool, a Romanesque affair with Ionic columns located on a cliff overlooking the sea, is so spectacular that it draws many non-guests who drop by for a look and drink. The 25 rooms and suites are also superb, large, and well-furnished with canopied beds and other antique pieces. Facilities and activities include a beach, two pools, horseback riding, and water sports. Expensive. 809/423-6220.

Ginger Bay Beach Club. The furnishings in the 16 suites in the three pink villlas at this bluff-top hotel with dramatic views of the ocean are more suited to the English hunt country than to the tropics. Despite that, this resort is lovely if you don't mind a 64-step walk down to the long beach on the Atlantic side of the island. Facilities include a pool and tennis courts. Expensive. 809/423-5810.

Glitter Bay. The Mediterranean-style villas house 88 beautifully furnished rooms on what once was the estate of Sir Edward Cunard, the cruise ship magnate. Cunard's great house has been expanded and is now used as the reception center while his coral-stone beach house, a replica of the Cunards' Venice palazzo, holds five wonderful suites. Facilities and activities include a beach, pool, tennis courts, and water sports. Very expensive. 809/422-4111.

Royal Pavilion. Glitter Bay's new sister resort, this pink palace is one of the most beautiful resorts we have visited. The grounds are lovingly landscaped, the night-lighting turns archways into dramatic stages, and the beach views are captivating. The 75 rooms are spacious and tastefully decorated, all with large balconies and patios. There is an attractive two-bedroom villa available, close to the tennis courts. Other facilities include a pool and water sports center. Very expensive. 809/422-5555.

Sandy Lane. In the early 1960s, Sandy Lane was the place to stay in Barbados. With a recent facelift, this lovely 115-room resort has regained much of its glamor. The rooms are large and tastefully furnished, and the beach is much wider here than at other resorts on the island. Facilities include a pool, tennis courts, and golf courses. Very expensive. 809/432-1311 or 800/223-3672.

For information about homes you can rent, please read Chapter 10, "A Villa of Your Own."

Dining and Nightlife

The dining rooms in the resorts serve excellent continental and West Indian dishes though the prices are a bit steep. The road along the west coast, where many of the resorts are located, is also home to numerous fine restaurants. Unfortunately, their prices are only a bit lower.

You will need to make dinner reservations at least a day ahead for the places listed below.

The following price categories for restaurants are for dinner for two, without wine or alcoholic beverages:

Inexpensive—$30 and less
Moderate—$30 to $50
Expensive—$50 to $100

Our choices:

Bagatelle Great House. Continental and West Indian cuisine are served in an elegant plantation great house. Expensive. 809/425-0666.

Carambola. Its creative menu features local seafood with innovative touches. Expensive. 809/432-0832.

La Cage aux Folles. Classic French cuisine is served in a colorful setting with fresh flowers and exotic parrots. Expensive. 809/432-1203.

Le Chateau Creole. Excellent Cajun and French cuisine is served in a romantic candlelit garden setting. Expensive. 809/422-4116.

Koko's. This old beachfront house serves some amazing West Indian dishes. Moderate. 809/424-4557.

Piperade. The open-air dining room at Glitter Bay features continental as well as West Indian dishes. Both are superb. Expensive. 809/422-4111.

Palm Terrace. One of the most dramatic dining rooms in the Caribbean, this Royal Pavilion restaurant serves fine continental and West Indian dishes in a setting that is absolutely stunning. Expensive. 809/422-4444.

Raffles. The West Indian dishes are among the best on the island. Expensive. 809/432-6557.

Seashell. This restaurant in the Sandy Lane Hotel has been winning awards for years for its fine Italian seafood dishes. Expensive. 809/432-1311.

For lunch, try the interesting Atlantis Hotel in Bathsheba on the rugged Atlantic Coast. The food, all classic Bajan dishes like fried flying fish, pickled bananas, and pumpkin fritters, is outstanding and inexpensive. The Wednesday and Sunday luncheon buffets are popular. Make reservations, though, for the porch. The indoor room is a bit dreary. 809/423-7350.

For nightlife, there are colorful and spectacular floor shows at the Plantation and Garden Theater (809/428-5048) every night from Thursday to Sunday, at the Royal Pavilion's Tabora's Restaurant (809/ 462-4444) on Wednesday, and at the Barbados Hilton (809/462-0200) on Sunday. Barbados! Barbados! is a popular musical comedy presented along with dinner at the Barbados Horticultural Society (809/ 435-6900).

For more information contact the Barbados Board of Tourism at 800 2nd Ave., New York, NY 10017, or call 212/986-6516. On the island, the tourist offices are on Harbour Road in Hastings (809/427-2623).

DOMINICA

Dominica is the island that most resembles the way all Caribbean islands once were.

Undeveloped and unspoiled, the 29- by 15-mile island has no casinos, shopping districts or large resorts. What Dominica has is an abundance of stunning natural wonders rarely found today. The island is a lush garden hosting a thick rain forest, hundreds of rivers and waterfalls, mountain lakes, a boiling lake that testifies to the volcanic past, and some of the highest peaks in the Caribbean.

Dominica (pronounced Dom-in-*ee*-ka) also has the only reservation on the islands for the Carib Indians, the peaceful inhabitants of the region whose numbers were decimated by the fierce Arawak Indians and the European colonists.

The natural wonders are what draws visitors to Dominica. The main town, Roseau, is home to about a fourth of the islands' 80,000 or so inhabitants. There are a few craft shops and cafés, but the important stop here is the National Park Service office on Victoria Street across from the Court House. There you can get numerous brochures, maps, and other materials on the island's wilderness.

Northeast of Roseau are the Sulphur Springs and Trafalgar Falls, a 20-story rush of water that is breathtaking.

Farther along the road is the Morne Trois Pitons, a tree-peak mountain whose highest point reaches 4,400 feet. This mountain and the adjacent 16,000-acre national park are filled with lush vegetation, wild flowers and orchids, huge versions of our house plants, lakes, and waterfalls. Among the more popular sights are the Freshwater Lake, where purple hyacinths bloom in the water, and the very rugged hiking trails that lead to the Boiling Lake and Valley of Desolation. The latter two attractions are reachable only after a difficult six-mile hike. Only lovers of volcanoes and geology may find this trek worthwhile.

North of the park is Emerald Pool, whose green banks are the result of the 60-foot waterfall spilling onto them.

The Atlantic Coast is where you will find the Carib Indian Reservation just north of the village of Castle Bruce. The reservation has been the Indians' home since 1903. They live simply, off the sea and land, but do sell their crafts on the reservation.

The other natural attractions worth a visit are Morne Diablotin, the island's highest peak (4,747 feet), and the Layou River Valley on the western half of the island. The rain forest covering Morne Diablotin's slopes is very green but so thick and dark that you should only enter it with a guide. The Layou River Valley is a fertile farmland, and the river itself offers many faces: placid pools, rushing rapids, and waterfalls.

Most of the beaches on the island are of dark sand. The best are Picard Beach on the northwest coast, Grand Bay just south of Roseau, and Paqua Bay on the Atlantic side.

Romantic Retreats

Accommodations are limited on the island. None of the resorts or hotels are grandly luxurious, but those mentioned below are charming.

The rates are for a room for two per night and do not include meals unless noted. The three categories:

Inexpensive—Less than $50
Expensive—$50 to $80
Very expensive—$80 and more

Meal plans are offered at many hotels and can help cut costs. All-inclusive plans offer all meals, snacks, drinks, wine, entertainment, activities, sports, gratuities, and airport transfers for one fee, which ranges from $1,000 to $3,000 per person per week. Whether that is a bargain depends on how much you eat, drink, and play, and whether you want more freedom to sample restaurants elsewhere on the island. Check your travel agent for current tariffs and the all-inclusive and other meal plans.

Our selections:

Evergreen Hotel. The 10 rooms in this quaint little inn are furnished simply, but tastefully. Expensive. 809/448-3288.

Papillote Wilderness Retreat. Nature-lovers will adore this seven-room rustic inn located in the middle of the rain forest. The guests share four bathrooms. Very expensive. 809/448-2287.

Reigate Hall. This 16-room inn, an alteration of what once was an eighteenth-century plantation house, is a dramatic and stunning retreat. The stone and hardwood building is located on a bluff, offering some striking views of the island and sea. All the rooms have balconies and tasteful decor. Amenities include a pool, tennis courts, sauna, and exercise room. Very expensive. 809/445-4031 and 800/223-9815.

Dining and Nightlife

The following price categories for restaurants are for dinner for two, without wine or alcoholic beverages:

Inexpensive—$30 and less
Moderate—$30 to $50
Expensive—$50 to $100

Our choices:

The Orchard. Get a table in the covered courtyard and feast on some of the best Creole food in the islands. Moderate. 809/448-3051.

La Robe Creole. Unusual menu at this cute Roseau dining room features dishes from seafood crepes to the local crab and coconut soup. The waitresses are dressed in Creole costumes. Expensive. 809/448-2896.

Papillote Wilderness Retreat. Dining at this lodge in the rain forest, if you are not a guest, requires some logistical work. The menu features popular island dishes, making the effort worthwhile.

Either hire a driver for the evening or stop for lunch during your daytime rambles. Moderate. 809/448-2287.

Reigate Hall. Superb French cuisine served at this elegant inn near Roseau. Expensive. 809/445-4031.

For nightlife, the Reigate Hall offers entertainment. Call for the schedule.

For more information contact the Dominica Tourist Board, Box 73, Roseau, Dominica, W. I. or call 809/448-2186. It's better to call if you are in a hurry. The mail takes forever.

GRENADA

The small island of Grenada, the most southern of the Windwards, is called the Isle of Spice. The name is well-taken, for the aroma of spices—cinnamon, nutmeg, mace, cocoa, and others—fills the air on this beautiful island.

The spices are grown on large plantations. Dougaldston Estate, near the town of Gouyave on the west coast, is where the spices are grown and processed. The women walking through the flats of spices are churning them to make sure they dry evenly.

The major city on the island is the capital, St. George's. This picturesque town is home to colorful buildings and seafront boulevards filled with shops, cafés, and markets.

The main street is Carenage, the road along the harbor. There you will find the shops, restaurants, and the tourist office where you can get maps of the island and town. From this boulevard, the passing parade of sailboats, schooners, and other vessels can become hypnotic.

The other major thoroughfare in St. George's is the Esplanade, the oceanfront road where Grencraft, the island's craft center, and other art galleries and boutiques may be found.

The center of activity in St. George's on Saturday mornings is the market on Granby Street just east of the Esplanade. Their local venders sell fruit, vegetables, crafts, and other items from 8:00 a.m. to 12:00 noon. Nearby, the fish market displays and sells the catch off the island's fishing boats.

Other attractions in St. George's include the Marryshow House at Tyrrel Street and Park Lane. The Victorian/West Indian mansion houses the Marryshow Folk Theatre, the island's cultural center. Plays, concerts, and other events are held there.

Out of town, the coast road leads north to the picturesque Conord Falls in the middle of mountains covered with bananas and other tropical fruit plantations. You can stop for a swim before continuing on to Gouyave, the spice town, where you turn west to the mountainous rain forest and the Grand Etang Lake and Visitors Center.

The park is a bird sanctuary and the lake is a mirror-like pool in the crater of a dormant volanco. Southeast of the lake is another dramatic waterfall. The Annandale Falls plunge 50 feet into a flower-filled glade.

The beautiful beaches on Grenada are Grand Anse, the main resort strip south of St. George's, and Mourne Rouge Beach south of Grand Anse. Levera Beach on the northern end is great for watching the Atlantic and Caribbean waves, but the surf is a bit too rough for swimming.

Grenada has two sister islands—Cariacou and Petit Martinique. If you really want to get away from it all, you can reach both islands by plane or boat. The scenery, particularly on Cariacou, is spectacular.

Romantic Retreats

There are no luxury resorts on Grenada, but there are many small and charming inns.

The rates are for a room for two per night and do not include meals unless noted. The three categories:

Inexpensive—Less than $100
Expensive—$100 to $200
Very expensive—$200 and more

Meal plans are offered at many hotels and can help cut costs. All-inclusive plans offer all meals, snacks, drinks, wine, entertainment, activities, sports, gratuities, and airport transfers for one fee, which ranges from $1,000 to $3,000 per person per week. Whether that is a bargain depends on how much you eat, drink, and play and whether you want more freedom to sample restaurants elsewhere on the island. Check your travel agent for current tariffs and the all-inclusive and other meal plans.

Our choices:

Blue Horizons Cottage Hotel. A five-minute walk from Grand Ansee beach, this lovely resort offers 36 suites and studios that are located in cottages scattered throughout a lush garden setting. Some suites have whirlpools and private swimming pools. Expensive. 809/444-4316.

Calabash. There are 22 large and well-furnished suites in this beachfront hotel where the maid prepares your breakfast to order and serves it in bed or on the patio. Amenities and activities include a garden-like setting, tennis courts, a pool, water sports, and a nearby yacht harbor. Very expensive. 809/444-4234.

Horse Shore Beach Hotel. The 18 suites in the Mediterranean-style hillside villas at this resort are furnished with antiques and magnificent carved-wood four-poster beds. Breakfast is prepared in the kitchen on your villa's patio and served outdoors, if you desire. There is a tiny beach, a pool, and water sports. Expensive. 809/444-4410 or 800/444-4244.

St. James Hotel. This century-old mansion in the quieter section of St. George's has 16 comfortable rooms, almost all with private baths. Amenities include a shuttle to Grand Anse beach. Inexpensive. 809/440-2041.

Secret Harbor Hotel. The 20 Mediterranean villas at this couples-only resort offer antique furnishings, four-poster beds, and stunning views from the balconies. Amenities include a small beach, tennis courts, a pool, and water sports. Very expensive. 809/444-4548.

Spice Island Inn. The 42 tastefully decorated suites on Grand Anse beach offer beautiful wicker and hardwood furnishings, enormous bathrooms, and privacy on enclosed patios. Ten of the villas have private plunge pools, 22 have whirlpools. Amenities include a pool and water sports. Very expensive. 809/444-4258 or 800/444-4423.

For information about homes you can rent, please read Chapter 10, "A Villa of Your Own."

Dining and Nightlife

The following price categories for restaurants are for dinner for two, without wine or alcoholic beverages:

Inexpensive—$30 and less

Moderate—$30 to $50
Expensive—$50 to $100

Our favorites:

La Belle Creole. Located at the Blue Horizons Cottage Hotel, this restaurant serves excellent West Indian fare. Moderate. 809/444-4316.

Betty Mascoll's Great House. The West Indian fare at this north shore home is worth the long drive from St. George's. Expensive. 809/440-9330.

Coconut's Beach. West Indian cuisine with a touch of France is offered in this beachfront restaurant in Gran Anse. Moderate. 809/444-4644.

Le Balisier. Creole seafood dishes are featured at this terrace restaurant offering stunning views of St. George's harbor. Moderate. 809/440-2346.

Mama's. Imagine what a West Indian diner in St. George's would look like, and you have Mama's. The local dishes are worth skipping elegant ambiance for an evening. Moderate. 809/444-1459.

St. James Hotel. Elegant setting and fine seafood are presented with a West Indian touch. Moderate. 809/444-2041.

Secret Harbour Hotel. This open-air dining room serves a fixed-price menu in perhaps the most elegant setting on the island. Expensive. 809/444-4439.

Spice Island Inn. This dining room is popular for its seafood and its Friday-night buffet with a steel band. Expensive. 809/444/-4258.

For nightlife, The Calabash and Spice Island inns offer live music in their lounges.

For more information contact the Grenada Tourist Office, Suite 701, 141 E. 44th St., New York, NY 10017, or call 212/687-9554 and 800/638-9852. On the island, the tourist office is on the Carenage in St. George's (809/440-2001).

MARTINIQUE

Close your eyes to the sea, the towering mountains, and the lush rain forest, and the island of Martinique could be mistaken for part of France's Côte d'Azur.

Politically, linguistically, culturally, Martinique is French. Like its sister islands in the French West Indies (St. Bart's, Guadeloupe and St. Martin), Martinique is a part of France. Not a possession, trust, or colony, but a full partner in all that is France.

The Arawak Indians called the island *Mandinina* (Island of Flowers), and the title is appropriate. The 50 by 22-mile island is a verdant wonderland, full of mountains, waterfalls, rivers, tropical plants, and exotic flowers.

The island's capital, Fort-de-France, is a hilly city whose narrow streets and pastel buildings with wrought-iron balconies resemble those of New Orleans. The tourist office is on the Boulevard Alfassa near the ferry docks. There you can pick up maps and other brochures on the island's attractions.

The major sights in town are the marketplace near the harbor where the usual assortment of crafts are sold; the Parc Floral et Culture where many specimens of the island's flowers are grown; and the Musée Departementale de Martinique on rue Blenac where artifacts from the Arawak and Carib Indians are displayed.

The main shopping district in this town is along rue Schoelcher. On that rue and along the side streets are numerous shops selling haute fashion, crafts, jewelry, and other luxury items.

Across the broad Baie de Fort-de-France is the village of Les Trois-Ilets. It is famous as the birthplace of Napoleon's wife, Empress Josephine, as well as for the fine craft items and baskets made and sold in the village. West of the village is the Musée de la Pagerie, a museum and memorial to Josephine. It is the kitchen of the estate on which she was born.

North of Fort-de-France is the small village of St-Pierre which, on May 8, 1902, became the Pompeii of the Caribbean when Mont Pelée erupted, killing all but one of the city's 30,000 inhabitants.

The ruins of the old city are open for tours and is the Musée Vulcanologique which commemorate the town and its tragic fate.

Four miles east of town on the slopes of Mont Pelée is Le Morne Rouge, a popular resort area for hikers, climbers, and other nature lovers.

The north end of the island holds the most spectacular drive along the six-mile road between Grand-Riviére and Macouba with stunning views of the sea.

The best beaches on Martinique are Anse-Trabaud on the Atlantic side, and Anse-Mitan and Les Salines on the Caribbean side. All beaches on the island are public, and topless sunbathing is common.

As lush as Martinique is, there is one place on the island that is unusual and very, very different from the rest of the island. Between Les Salines and Anse-Trabaud is a forbidding zone, a petrified forest that is out of place on the garden spot of France.

Romantic Retreats

The rates are for a room for two per night and do not include meals unless noted. The three categories:

Inexpensive—Less than $100
Expensive—$100 to $200
Very expensive—$200 and more

Meal plans are offered at many hotels and can help cut costs. All-inclusive plans offer all meals, snacks, drinks, wine, entertainment, activities, sports, gratuities, and airport transfers for one fee ranging from $1,000 to $3,000 per person per week. Whether that is a bargain depends on how much you eat, drink, and play, and whether you want more freedom to sample restaurants elsewhere on the island. Check your travel agent for current tariffs and the all-inclusive and other meal plans.

Our favorites:

Le Bakoua. The furnishings in the 140 rooms in this hillside resort facing a beach are comfortable though simply furnished. A pool, tennis courts, and water sports are available. Very expensive. 596/66-02-02.

La Bateliére Hotel and Casino. The 207 rooms in this beachfront hotel are spacious and furnished with all the modern necessities. Amenities include casino, pool, tennis courts, sauna, and water sports. Very expensive. 596/61-49-49.

Hotel Plantation de Leyritz. This restored eighteenth-century plantation is a charming retreat located in a mountainside tropical garden and banana plantation. The four rooms in the main house are comfortable and furnished with antiques, while the 49 other rooms are more rustic and are located in a restored carriage house, cabins, and other buildings. Facilities include a spa, fitness center, stables, tennis courts, and a pool. Expensive. 596/78-53-92.

Manoir de Beauregard. Furnished with items from the cathedral of Fort-de-France, this 275-year-old house sits on 50 acres of lovely grounds. The manor house has 15 antique-filled rooms while the stone hillside villa has eight antique-filled suites. A pool, bicycles, and nearby beach are available. Expensive. 596/76-73-40 or 800/223-6510.

Le Méridien Trois-Ilets. There are 303 luxurious rooms in this large, modern, beachfront resort. Great views, lovely gardens, and spacious rooms. Facilities and activities include a pool, tennis courts, marina, casino, and water sports. Very expensive. 596/66-00-00 or 800/543-4300.

St. Aubin Hotel. This restored Victorian on the Atlantic coast has 15 spacious modern rooms with stunning views of the Atlantic. There is a pool. Expensive. 596/69-34-77 or 800/223-9815.

For information about homes you can rent, please read Chapter 10, "A Villa of Your Own."

Dining and Nightlife

Dining in Martinique is wonderful. There are numerous fine restaurants serving a blend of Creole and classic French cuisine.

The following price categories for restaurants are for dinner for two without wine or alcoholic beverages:

Inexpensive—$30 and less
Moderate—$30 to $50
Expensive—$50 to $100
Very expensive—More than $100

Our favorites:

Aux Filets Bleus. This casual dining spot on the beach in Pointe Marin features fresh seafood. Moderate. 596/76-73-42.

La Belle Epoque. French, but with a West Indian accent, is the cuisine at this intimate (nine tables) restaurant in a turn-of-the-century manor house in Fort-de-France. Expensive. 596/64-01-09.

Diamant Creole. The Creole seafood dishes are stunning in this small Fort-de-France house with only seven tables. Moderate. 596/73-18-25.

La Fontane. Surrounded by trees, this lovely Victorian-style house in Fort-de-France is filled with flowers, antiques, and oriental rugs. The classic French dishes are likewise superb. Expensive. 596/64-28-70.

La Grand 'Voile. Excellent French cuisine with a Creole touch is served in an elegant room overlooking the harbor in Fort-de-France. Expensive. 596/70-29-29.

La Villa Creole. Which is the biggest attraction here? The lush garden, or the superb Creole and French dishes, or popular owner/singer Guy Dawson, who entertains during dinner at this Trois-Ilet restaurant? All three make this a special place. Moderate. 596/66-05-53.

Le Tiffany. Dine by candelight on the terrace or in the intimate antique-filled room in this popular and elegant Fort-de-France restaurant. The magic is found not only in the superb Creole dishes, but also in the shows every Friday night. Expensive. 596/71-33-82.

For nightlife, Les Grand Ballets de Martinique, a troupe of singers, dancers, and musicians rotate around among the Bakoue, La Bateliére, and Méridien hotels. The major hotels have entertainment most nights during the high season.

For nightclubs and discos, try Le Sweety (no phone) and Le New Hippy (596/71-74-60) in Fort-de-France. The island's two casinos are the Casino Trois-Inlets in the Méridien Hotel (596/66-00-00) and La Bateliére (596/61-49-49). Both charge admission.

For more information contact the French West Indies Tourist Office at 610 5th Ave., New York, NY 10020 or call 212/757-1125. On the island, the tourist offices are on Blvd. Alfassa in Fort-de-France (596/63-79-60).

ST. LUCIA

One word sums up this small Windward island, "Beautiful."

The 27- by 13-mile oval island of St. Lucia has some of the most stunning scenery in the Caribbean. The southwest coast is a rugged landscape of green so filled with beautiful vegetation and scenic spots that comparisons with some of Hawaii's gorgeous scenery springs to mind.

On the southwest coast are the two main landmarks that will lock this island forever in a visitor's mind: Les Pitons, the two conical volcanic peaks at water's edge that soar almost a half-mile above the oceanfront. The view of the Pitons (Gros and Petite) is stunning whether you approach them over the twisting, difficult, coastal road or the easier way by sea.

The Pitons are not the only evidence of St. Lucia's volcanic past. Near the coastal town of Soufriére are the Diamond Falls and Mineral Baths which are fed from sulphur springs. The baths were built with the assistance of France's Louis XVI who thought they would help his troops in the region recuperate.

The baths were sacked in the afternoon of the French Revolution and were only recently restored and opened to the public. The path to the falls is through a tropical rain forest garden, filled with marvelous flowering plants and trees.

South of town is La Soufriére, billed as the world's only drive-in volcano. There's no lava here, but pools of bubbling mud and water emit forth the sulphur fumes that give the volcano and town their names.

North of the Pitons, through the rain forest and banana plantations, is Marigot Bay, one of the Caribbean's most scenic harbors.

The capital of St. Lucia is Castries, a bustling and clean city that is the business and export center of the island. There are few historic buildings in Castries which was almost completely destroyed during a tragic fire in 1948.

One survivor worth a visit is the majestic stone Cathedral of the Immaculate Conception, built in 1897 on the edge of the city's park called Columbus Square.

There are a few shops in Castries, but the main shopping area is the Market at Jeremie and Peynier streets where island residents sell fruit, crafts, and other items both inside the red-roof market or on the sidewalks surrounding it.

Duty free shops can be found across the harbor at the new Mediterranean-style complex called Point Seraphine where the cruise ships dock. The 23 shops and restaurants here are either empty when there are no ships in port or crammed when the ships are in. Take a look, but better bargains on local goods can be found in the Market in town.

The best-known shop on the island is Bagshaws of St. Lucia, whose colorful sports clothes for women and children are popular throughout the Caribbean. There is a Bagshaws shop at the Point Seraphine Complex, but the best store is the original on the bluff above the north end of the beach at the Hotel La Toc. There you can shop, see how the items are made, and catch some stunning views of the coastline.

The best beaches on St. Lucia are on the west coast where the surf is gentler than the rough Atlantic side. However, because driving down the west coast takes far more time than you can imagine, don't head to the Pitons or the beaches there unless you are making a day of it. Vigie Beach, north of Castries, and Pigeon Point, an island that is now a national park and connected to the mainland by a bridge, have fine beaches.

Also on the north end is a small village that is a must-stop if you are on the island on a Friday night. On those nights, Gros Inlet becomes one big block party with music, dancing, and vendors selling food and crafts along the streets of the town.

Romantic Retreats

The rates are for a room for two per night and do not include meals unless noted. The three categories:

Inexpensive—Less than $100
Expensive—$100 to $200
Very expensive—$200 and more

Meal plans are offered at many hotels and can help cut costs. All-inclusive plans offer all meals, snacks, drinks, wine, entertainment, activities, sports, gratuities, and airport transfers for one fee ranging from $1,000 to $3,000 per person per week. Whether that is a bargain depends on how much you eat, drink, and play, and whether you want more freedom to sample restaurants elsewhere on the island. Check your travel agent for current tariffs and the all-inclusive and other meal plans.

Our Choices:

Anse Chastanet Beach Hotel. This isolated hotel just north of the imposing Gros Piton offers 25 rooms in octagonal cottages hidden away in the tropical forest on the hill above the beach and another 12 in new beachfront villas. Popular with divers, sailors, and couples seeking solitude, this resort also offers a nice beach of light-grey sand, tennis courts, and watersports. Expensive. 809/454-7355.

Cunard Hotel La Toc and La Toc Suites. The island's finest, this resort is made up of a pink hotel with 192 rooms (some of which are being redone into pleasant suites) and 54 rooms in the pastel-colored villas along a hilly peninsula a few steps south of the main hotel. The villas offer dramatic scenery, spacious rooms, private housekeeping services, VCRs, and in some, private plunge pools. Amenities include tennis courts, golf courses, two pools, a fitness center, numerous spots in which you can sit and enjoy the view, nightclub (including a lively Saturday night floor show), and water sports. A candidate for the most beautiful resort we have visited. Very expensive. 809/452-3081 or 800/222-0939.

Marigot Bay Resort. There are 47 rooms in the inn, villas, and hotel in this isolated resort on perhaps the loveliest harbor in the Caribbean. The isolation makes it popular with sailors, divers, and those seeking a romantic and beautiful hideaway. Accommodations are spacious and comfortable. Facilities and activities include a dive shop, sailing charters, and other water sports. Very expensive. 809/453-4357 or 800/535-7289.

Windjammer Landing. The 50 villas of white stucco and terra cotta roofs and trim are stunning at this new hillside resort. The rooms are spacious and include kitchenettes, plunge pools, and balconies. Amenities include a small beach, water sports, squash, and racquet ball. Expensive. 80/223-1588.

For information about homes you can rent, please read Chapter 10, "A Villa of Your Own."

Dining and Nightlife

If you stay at Marigot Bay or Anse Chastanet, the long and difficult drive to Castries and the restaurants there is not worth the effort.

The following price categories for restaurants are for dinner for two, without wine or alcoholic beverages:

Inexpensive—$30 and less
Moderate—$30 to $50
Expensive—$50 to $100

Green Parrot. This lively restaurant on Morne Fortune, the hill overlooking Castries, serves some fine continental dishes. Go on Wednesday and Saturday nights when limbo and calypso shows are presented. Moderate. 809/452-3399.

Les Pitons. The elegant open-air dining room at La Toc serves continental and French dishes that do not live up to the surroundings. Expensive. 809/452-3081.

San Antoine's. Also on Morne Fortune, this restored nineteenth-century house overlooking the harbor features haute cuisine, an extensive menu, and a very elegant atmosphere. Expensive. 809/452-4660.

Rain. An old Victorian house across from Columbus Square in Castries, this popular restaurant serves fine Creole food. Moderate. 809/452-3022.

For nightlife, the fishing village of Gros Inlet and its carnival atmosphere is the place to be on Friday night. Popular nightclubs include Splash in the St. Lucian Hotel (809/452-8351), and the Halcyon Wharf Disco at the Laycon Beach Club (809/452-5331). Cunard Hotel La Toc offers a fine floor show on Saturday nights.

For more information contact the St. Lucia Tourist Board, 820 Second Ave., Ninth Floor, New York, NY 10017, or call 212/867-2950. On the island, the tourist offices are in the Point Seraphine shopping complex and on Jeremies Street in Castres. The number for both offices is 809/452-5968.

ST. VINCENT AND THE GRENADINES

If the Caribbean has a high-rent district, the 33 islands that comprise St. Vincent and the Grenadines are it. On these shores may be found elegant villas and grand resorts. These man-made attractions are overshadowed, at least on St. Vincent, by the magnificant vegetation and the remarkable coral reefs and marine life in the crystal-clear waters.

St. Vincent, 18 by 11 miles, is the largest island in this group. The capital is Kingstown on the southeast coast. The capital's attractions include Bay Street, famed for its craft shops and its Market where fish, fruit, vegetables, and other items are sold on Saturday mornings.

Two historic churches on Back Street are worth a visit. St. George's Cathedral and St. Mary's Roman Catholic Cathedral were both built in the early nineteenth-century and offer a contrast in architectural styles.

The best sights are outside town. The 240-year-old Botanical Gardens just outside town and the nearby Montreal Gardens are lush and filled with exotic flowers, orchids, spice trees, and other plants. East of the Montreal Gardens is the Mesopotamia Region, an area of thick forests, banana plantations that stretch east to St. Vincent's rugged and beautiful Atlantic coast.

The best beaches on this island are at Buccament Bay and Questelle's Bay where you will find black sand.

Before leaving St. Vincent, take a boat ride to the north coast to the Falls of Baleine which are difficult to reach by land. The boat will take you to the beach which is only a short hike from the six-story falls almost hidden in the forest.

The Grenadines provide a sharp contrast to St. Vincent. These islands are small, offering a lot of privacy and little commercial development. Only five of the 32 Grenadines are developed enough to warrant mentioning. Here is a brief rundown: Bequia is popular with divers who find wide varieties of marine life; Mayreau is an agricultural island, offering uncrowded beaches and small inns; Palm Island is a one-resort island; and Mustique and Petit St. Vincent are popular with the Rich and Famous.

Romantic Retreats

The rates are for a room for two per night, and do not include meals unless noted. The three categories:

Inexpensive—Less than $100
Expensive—$100 to $200
Very expensive—$200 and more

Meal plans are offered at many hotels and can help cut costs. All-inclusive plans offer all meals, snacks, drinks, wine, entertainment, activities, sports, gratuities, and airport transfers for one fee ranging from $1,000 to $3,000 per person per week. Whether that is a bargain depends on how much you eat, drink, and play, and whether you want more freedom to sample restaurants elsewhere on the island. Check your travel agent for current tariffs and the all-inclusive and other meal plans.

Our choices on St. Vincent:

Cobblestone Inn. There are 19 spacious and comfortable rooms in this early nineteenth-century stone warehouse in the city. The beach is three miles away. Inexpensive. 809/456-1937.

Emerald Valley Resort. The accommodations in the 12 chalets are simple, but the mountain setting is beautiful in this resort. Facilities include a casino, tennis courts, volleyball courts, croquet courts, and pool. Expensive. 809/458-7421.

Grand View Beach Hotel. The location is stunning: a blufftop garden of palms, flowering trees, and bougainvillaea. The 12 rooms in this large, white, two-story hotel are pleasant and simply furnished. Expensive. 809/458-4811.

Young Island. This private, 36-acre island sits only a few hundred yards off the main island. This is a wonderful resort, perfect for that isolated hideaway. The 29 rooms are located in cottages set amid lush hillside gardens. Amenities include a brilliant white-sand beach, tennis courts, scuba diving pool, and water sports. Very expensive. 809/458-4826 or 800/223-1108.

On Bequia:

Frangipani Hotel. This West Indies inn is the center of the island social life and gossip. There are eight spacious rooms in the stone-and-wood garden cottages which have private baths, while the three in the main house share facilities. Furnishings are simple but adequate. Facilities and activities include tennis courts, yacht services, and water sports. Expensive. 809/458-3255.

Friendship Bay Hotel. This beachfront resort has 12 acres of lovely gardens and 27 beautiful rooms in the white hotel and the coral stone villas near the water. Amenities include a beach and water sports. Expensive. 809/458-3222.

Spring on Bequia. Set in a hillside orchard or tropical fruit, this modern—almost avant-garde—hotel offers 11 comfortable rooms. The beach is a mile away, but a pool and tennis courts are available at this hotel. Expensive. 809/458-3414.

On Mayreau:

Salt Whistle Bay Club. The island's best (and only) hotel, with five cottages, one suite, and eight small rooms built and furnished by island craftsmen. It's rustic, but the peace is heavenly. That's because the only other people on the island are the 170 residents of the village on the hill. Amenities include windsurfing, water sports, and boat chartering. Very expensive. 416/430-1275.

On Mustique:

The Cotton House. This is casual elegance at its best. The 30 rooms in the restored eighteenth-century Georgian house and its three guest cottages are beautifully furnished. Amenities include stables, pristine beaches, water sports, and tennis courts. Very expensive. 809/456-4777 or 212/696-1323.

On Palm Island:

The Palm Island Beach Club. The 24 rooms in the 12 stone cottages are colorful and tastefully done with wicker. This is a very private resort for couples looking for casual elegance and isolation. It has an extensive water sports and fitness center. Very expensive. 809/458-4804.

On Petit St. Vincent:

The 113-acre private island is the resort, offering superb food, 22 stone cottages, and absolute privacy (You want something, raise a flag, or even two red flags for complete privacy). Facilities include tennis courts, water sports center, and fitness trails. Very expensive. 809/458-4801 and 513/242-1333.

For information about homes you can rent, please read Chapter 10, "A Villa of Your Own."

Dining and Nightlife

The only restaurants we list are on St. Vincent, Bequia, and Mustique. Dining on the other Grenadine islands is so limited that the resorts we listed above are also the best (and sometimes the only) place to dine.

The following price categories for restaurants are for dinner for two, without wine or alcoholic beverages:

Inexpensive—$30 and less
Moderate—$30 to $50
Expensive—$50 to $100

On St. Vincent:

French Restaurant. This open-air restaurant in Villa Beach serves fine seafood and other classic French dishes. Expensive. 809/458-4972.

Mariner's Inn. This casual spot offers excellent West Indian fare and a Friday night dance party. Moderate. 809/458-4287.

Young Island. Prepare yourself for lavish feasts with whole roast pigs, seafood, and other meats. Expensive. 809/458-4826.

For nightlife, try the Attic, a jazz club in Kingstown (809/457-2558).

On Bequia:

Daphne's. Spicy Creole and curried dishes make this West Indian spot very special. Moderate. 809/458-3271.

Frangipani. Waterside dining here features the best of local seafood. Moderate. 809/458-3255.

La Petit Jardin. This dining room offers elegant service, classic French cuisine with a hint of the Indies. Expensive. 809/458-3318.

On Mustique:

Basils Beach Bar. Gathering place for sailors and the occupants of the island's lavish villas, this restaurant has lots of atmosphere and great seafood. Expensive. 809/458-4621.

For more information contact the St. Vincent and Grenadines Tourist Office at 801 2nd Ave., 21st Floor, New York, NY 10017, or call 212/687-4981. On St. Vincent, the tourist offices are on Egmont Street in Kingstown (809/457-1502).

The Divi Divi Beach Resort on Aruba.

CHAPTER 4

The Southern Caribbean

JUST OFF THE COAST of Venezuela, five southern Caribbean islands are a study in contrasts.

The Netherlands Antilles—Aruba, and Bonaire and Curaçao—offer almost every attraction a traveler could desire, but just not on the same island. The big luxurious resorts and the glamorous nightspots are found on Aruba; exotic wildlife and sensational diving are found on Bonaire; and the architectural beauty of eighteenth-century Amsterdam is found on Curaçao.

The two former British colonies in the southern Caribbean—Trinidad and Tobago—also offer two different faces. Trinidad is where Carnival originated and its large capital is a lively city offering numerous attractions for visitors. Tobago is less developed and attracts those seeking the delights of nature and the absence of crowds.

ARUBA

The interior of this 70-square-mile island is an eerie landscape of rock, cactus, abandoned gold mines, and uninhabited Indian caves. In this stark forbidding landscape, it's hard to imagine that just a few miles away, on the western coast, one of the Caribbean's largest parties is taking place.

On the western coast are Aruba's dozen-plus large resorts, casinos, and nightclubs; where every night is an excuse for a party—limbo contests, lively concerts, beach cookouts, or just a good time—at the nightspots.

The resorts congregate on this coast for the lovely beaches there. The best sands on the west side are at Manchebo Beach (topless optional), Palm Beach (behind the American Aruba Hotel, with water sports facilities) and Eagle beach (between Manchebo and Palm and perhaps the least crowded). Our favorite beach on Aruba is also the most beautiful, Boca Prince, a tiny east coast beach flanked by rugged cliffs and graced by large waves. It's stunning!

Off the beaches, the small capital city of Oranjestad is home to some beautiful eighteenth-century Dutch architectures on Wilheminastraat and a variety of the usual duty-free shops on Nassaustraat.

Though the official language is Dutch, the friendly residents of the island speak English and a local patois made of many other languages.

For an inland tour, hire a taxi and take a driving tour of the mines, caves, and cacti wonderlands. Wait until you are burned, though, for the tour isn't as glamorous as the shore.

Romantic Retreats

All the hotels on the island are on the west coast and, compared to the rest of the Caribbean, are surprisingly reasonable, although larger and less intimate.

The rates are for a room for two persons per night and do not include meals unless noted. The three categories:

Inexpensive—Less than $75
Expensive—$75 to $125
Very expensive—$125 and more

Meal plans are offered at many hotels and can help cut costs. All-inclusive plans offer all meals, snacks, drinks, wine, entertainment, activities, sports, gratuities, and airport transfers for one fee, which ranges from $1,000 to $3,000 per person per week. Whether that is a bargain depends on how much you eat, drink, and play and whether you want more freedom to sample restaurants elsewhere on the island. Check your travel agent for current tariffs and the all-inclusive and other meal plans.

Our choices:

Americana Aruba Hotel & Casino. This luxurious, 406-room, beachfront high-rise offers spacious rooms and enough activities to keep you busy day and night. Amenities include a casino, nightclub, pool, tennis courts, water sports, and nightly entertainment. Expensive. 297/8-24500 or 800/223-1588.

Divi Divi Beach Resort. Casual but stylish, this 200-room hotel has one of the greatest white-sand beaches in the Caribbean. It offers a variety of comfortable rooms, with the most romantic ones being the casitas (cottages). There are 110 rooms in the low-rise main building, 40 more in small casitas, and another 50 in a new Divi Dos section facing the beach. Amenities include the beach, two pools, tennis courts, jacuzzi, nightly entertainment (plus a nearby casino), and water sports. Expensive. 297/8-23300 or 800/367-DIVI.

Divi Tamarijn Beach Resort. This casual beachfront resort has 206 rooms in two-story, townhouse-style buildings. The rooms are nice, but not exceptional. The pace here is very slow and casual. Amenities include a pool, tennis courts, and activities. Expensive. 800/367-DIVI.

Golden Tulip Aruba Caribbean Resort & Casino. Perhaps the resort with the longest name in the Caribbean, this fashionable 400-

room, newly renovated, palace-like resort has played host to the Queen of Holland and Elizabeth Taylor. The rooms are beautifully furnished and have ocean views. Facilities include a casino, pool, nightclub, tennis courts, fitness center, and shops. Expensive. 297/8-33555 or 800/344-1212.

(Aruba is one of the few islands in this book without any villas for visitors to rent).

Dining and Nightlife

Dining on Aruba is a great bargain, with a fine meal often costing under $25 per person. Reservations are a must.

The following price categories for restaurants are for dinner for two, without wine or alcoholic beverages:

Inexpensive—$10 and less
Moderate—$10 to $20
Expensive—$30 and more

Our choices:

Chez Mathilde. This distinguished restaurant in a nineteenth-century home in Oranjestad is an international mixture: the chef is Swiss, the menu is French, and the setting is Old Dutch. The food is as wonderful as the elegant setting. Expensive. 297/8-34968.

Papiamento. Another intimate restaurant where the location—this time in a house with stylish decor, a beautiful garden, and stunning views—is as wonderful as the superb food. One star is the mixed seafood which is grilled on the table on a heated stone in this Oranjestad spot. Expensive. 297/8-4544.

Bali Floating Restaurant. We have several rules about restaurants. Never dine in a restaurant that promises "Home Cooking" (if it was so great at home then why are you eating out?) or one that is located on the top of a building or on a boat. This restaurant,

A Real Damper

Now matter how interesting the island, one thing will ruin your vacation: rain.

The rainy season in the Caribbean and the south Atlantic is the fall, at the end of the hurricane season, which runs from June through October. The storms then can dump large amounts of rain, but usually last no more than a day or so.

At other times of the year, short-lived storms can chase you from the beach. That happened to us on more than one occasion, and our attempts to get a weather forecast from various locals-in-the-know proved unenlightening.

When we asked when the sunshine would return, the answer was always the same. "Tomorrow."

Finally, after three days of scrabble games and island touring, we asked a tourist official about the consistently wrong forecast of "Sunshine tomorrow."

"Ah," she explained with a smile. "When it rains we just call it liquid sunshine.

however, is the exception. This Oriental-style houseboat in Oranjestad harbor serves superb Indonesian food. Moderate. 297/8-22131.

Boonoonoonoos. Don't pronounce it, just sit down and enjoy some of the excellent Caribbean dishes at this Oranjestad dining room. Moderate. 297/8-31888.

La Dolce Vita. Acclaimed by *Gourmet* magazine, this Italian restaurant located in a private house in Oranjestad is known for its seafood, veal, and pasta. Expensive. 297/8-25675.

Papagao Restaurant. Excellent northern Italian cuisine is served in a remarkable setting blending the beauty of the Oranjestad waterfront with the lush vegetation of a jungle. Expensive. 297/8-24140.

This is the island for nightlife. The Alhambra Casino (297/8-25434), the Aruba Concorde (297/8-24466), the Golden Tulip (297/

8-33555), and the Aruba Palm Beach Hotel (297/8-23900) are the most popular.

For dancing and music, try Le Visage (297/8-35000), Club Scaramouche (297/8-24954), or Stellaris Club in the American Aruba Hotel (297/8-24500), where you can have dinner and enjoy the show.

The Aruba Dance Theater (297/8-33555) at the Golden Tulip Hotel is a lively nightclub dance-and-music revue. It's held every Saturday and you can dine there in the Pelican terrace during the show.

For more information contact the Aruba Tourism Authority at 1270 Avenue of the Americas, Suite 2212, New York, NY 10020 or call 212/246-3030 or 800/TO-ARUBA. On the island, the tourist office is at A. Schuttestraat 2, opposite the wharf in Oranjestad (297/8-23777).

BONAIRE

Home to exotic birds and rare plants, little Bonaire is quite an interesting island, but is not for every traveler. The landscape is that of a desert, the beaches are small, and the resorts are limited. But if you like scuba diving, snorkeling, and bird-watching, you will be in paradise.

Bonaire has exceptional diving, perhaps the best in the Caribbean. The Bonaire Marine Park, stretching the entire coastline, has coral reefs that are home to an amazing and colorful array of undersea life. The entire island is a reef, having been submerged entirely more than once during its existence.

The underwater sights are so fantastic that they overshadow Bonaire's beautiful beaches, which come in a variety of colors. The best are Boca Cocolishi (on the north), where the sand is black; Boca Slagbaai (on the northwest), where the sand is white; and the appropriately named Pink Beach (on the southwestern coast). At all of these, the water is crystal-clear and the sands, except on weekends, are deserted.

Elsewhere, the island's 122 square miles also feature exotic geography, unusual plants, and numerous species of rare and beautiful birds. Lovers of nature and fantastic scenery should visit Washington/Slagbaai Park, a 15,000-acre game preserve featuring cacti, reptiles, and wild mammals. More than 100 species of birds, including flamingos, live in this public parkland.

Bonaire's capital, Kralendjik, is a picture-perfect city, with clean street and cute, pastel-colored houses and buildings. It has only 2,500 residents and only one main street, Breedestraat. There you will find shops and restaurants, but little else of significance except the Insituto Folklore Bonaire and its small collection.

Romantic Retreats

This is a divers' island, and all of these resorts have extensive diving facilities.

The rates are for a room for two per night and do not include meals unless noted. The three categories:

Inexpensive—Less than $75
Expensive—$75 to $125
Very expensive—$125 and more

Meal plans are offered at many hotels and can help cut costs. All-inclusive plans offer all meals, snacks, drinks, wine, entertainment, activities, sports, gratuities, and airport transfers for one fee, which ranges from $1,000 to $3,000 per person per week. Whether that is a bargain depends on how much you eat, drink, and play and whether you want more freedom to sample restaurants elsewhere on the island. Check your travel agent for current tariffs and the all-inclusive and other meal plans.

Our choices:

Cap'n Don's Habitat. Cap'n Don is owner, diver extraordinaire, colorful character, and chief instigator when things become too quiet at this 27-room resort offering some of the finest rooms on Bonaire. Take your pick of the new apartments, villas, or the charming older cottages. Amenities include bicycles, a dive shop, and photo labs. This is a casual and relaxed resort. Expensive. 599/7-8290 or 800/223-5581.

Divi Flamingo Beach Hotel & Casino. There are 100 rooms at the oceanfront resort, featuring one of the most respected dive shops on the island. Facilities include a very casual casino, two pools, and photo labs. Expensive. 599/7-8285 or 800/367-3484.

Sorobon Beach Resort. Not for everyone, this 25-cottage resort attracts "naturalists"—i.e., nudists—mainly from Europe. Expect about half of the guests to be underdressed. Facilities include a water sports center. Expensive. 599/7-8738.

For information about homes you can rent, please read Chapter 10, "A Villa of Your Own."

Dining and Nightlife

The following price categories for restaurants are for dinner for two, without wine or alcoholic beverages:

Inexpensive—$30 and less
Moderate—$30 to $50
Expensive—$50 to $100

Our choices:

Bistro des Amis. The creative menu at this intimate French restaurant will tantalize you, but stick with the house specials. Expensive. 599/7-8003.

Den Laman Aquarium Bar & Restaurant. Don't feel guilty when you order seafood and then look up to see a cousin of your entrée swimming peacefully in the huge aquarium that holds sharks and tropical fish. Stick with the Creole dishes with seafood. Expensive. 599/7-8955.

Le Chic. Lives up to its name as the most elegant restaurant on the island. Terrific seafood with French sauces. Expensive. 599/7-8617.

Mona Lisa Bar & Restaurant. Indonesian and Dutch fare served in a hangout for locals. Moderate. 599/7-8718.

For nightlife, other than films and slide shows on coral reefs and diving, try the casinos at the Flamingo Beach Hotel (599/7-8285) or the Black Coral Casino at the Bonaire Beach Hotel (599/7-8448).

The most popular disco is E Wowo at Kaya L.D. Gerharts and Kaya Grandi in Kralendijk.

For more information contact the Bonaire Government Tourist Office at 275 7th Ave., 19th floor, New York, NY 10001 or call 212/242-7707. On the island, the tourist office is on Kaya Grandi in Kralendijk (599/7-8322).

CURAÇAO

Larger than its sister islands of Aruba and Bonaire, cosmopolitan Curaçao enchants visitors with its excellent reef diving and its colorful waterfront homes that recreate images of Holland.

The Dutch settlers have made the 38-mile by 7-mile island a tropical version of Holland, duplicating the Netherlands' friendly reception for visitors as well as the culture and architecture.

Willemstad, a challenger to Charlotte Amalie for "shopping capital" of the Caribbean, is a city divided by the entrance to its busy harbor in Santa Anna Bay. The channel is lined with thick ramparts once used to defend the bay from attackers.

From the Otrabanda side of the water, the pastel-colored homes of the capital offer a visual delight for travellers. These waterfront homes, many more than a century old, are among the more beautiful sights in the Caribbean.

Across the waterway, the Punda region of Willemstad is where you will see the Floating Market, where the Venezuelan ships sell their produce and catches, the Scharloo district's old mansions built by many of the first Jewish colonialists, and the Mikveh Israel-Emanual Synagogue, built in 1650 and still in use. It is the oldest temple in the western hemisphere.

Willemstad's famed shopping is concentrated along Heerenstraat, Madurostraat, Gomezplein, and Breedestraat. The Waterfort Arches on the Plaza Piar offers the choicest collection of shops in the city.

Outside Willemstad, the landscape is dotted with unusual cacti, aloe, and divi divi trees. You may even see a few of the classic Dutch windmills. Two other popular attractions are on the eastern coast, where you can visit the Curaçao Seaquarium and the Curaçao Underwater Park, 12.5 miles of reef for divers.

Many of the 38 beaches on the island are small and located in hard-to-find coves. The best are Santa Barbara Beach on the southeast coast, which is more like a party than a sunbathing spot; Blauw Bay near Willemstad; and Daai Booi Bay, farther to the west.

Romantic Retreats

Curaçao doesn't have many fancy resorts, but does have some nice places offering rooms at reasonable prices.

The rates are for a room for two per night and do not include meals unless noted. The three categories:

Inexpensive—Less than $75
Expensive—$75 to $100
Very expensive—$100 and more

Meal plans are offered at many hotels and can help cut costs. All-inclusive plans offer all meals, snacks, drinks, wine, entertainment, activities, sports, gratuities, and airport transfers for one fee, which ranges from $1,000 to $3,000 per person per week. Whether that is a bargain depends on how much you eat, drink, and play and whether you want more freedom to sample restaurants elsewhere on the island. Check your travel agent for current tariffs and the all-inclusive and other meal plans.

Our choices:

Avila Beach Hotel. This stately, 200-year-old mansion has hosted the Royal family of the Netherlands, attracting them with the meticulous service, classical concerts, the best beach on the island, and excellent dining. The 87 rooms and 20 apartments are comfortable and are decorated in Scandinavian modern. Expensive. 599/961-4377.

Curaçao Plaza Hotel & Casino. This hotel has a unique distinction; it's the only one in the Caribbean (and perhaps the world) that must carry marine collision insurance. That's because the 245-room lxuxury high rise, built into the seventeenth-century ramparts guarding the entrance to St. Ann's Harbor, is very close to the water. The rooms are spacious and attractive. Facilities include pool, nightclub, and casino. Expensive. 599/961-2500.

Golden Tulip Coral Cliff Resort and Beach Club. The secluded beach at this 35-room resort attracts sunbathers and birdwatchers alike. The hillside rooms are simple and overlook the sea. Facilities include a small casino, pool, marina, dive shop, and water sports center. Expensive. 599/964-1610 or 800/233-9815.

Princess Beach Hotel and Casino. The 203 huge rooms in this beachfront resort offer simply stunning views. Facilities include a windsurfing school, pool, spa, dive shop, tennis courts, pool, sauna, and free shuttle to town. Expensive. 599/961-4944 or 800/233-9815.

For information about homes you can rent, please read Chapter 10, "A Villa of Your Own."

Dining and Nightlife

Many of Curaçao's restaurants are in romantic old homes. Call for reservations during high season. Dress is usually casual.

The following price categories for restaurants are for dinner for two, without wine or alcoholic beverages:

Inexpensive—$20 and less
Moderate—$20 to $35
Expensive—$35 and more

Our choices:

Bistro Le Clochard. Built into the side of the eighteenth-century Fort Rif, this dark romantic dining room serves up some stunning French and Swiss dishes. Live music, some nights. Expensive. 599/962-5666.

De Taveerne. The antique-filled dining rooms in this nineteenth-century country mansion are beautiful; perfect for a romantic dinner in which seafood ranks highly. Expensive. 599/97-0669.

La Bistroelle. This beautiful country inn offers French seafood dishes that are as divine as the decor. Expensive. 599/97-6929.

Rijsstaffel Indonesia Restaurant. The Rijsstaffel is a feast, featuring anywhere from one to three dozen exotic dishes. Expensive. 599/961-2999.

For nightlife, the casinos in the Curaçao Plaza Hotel (599/961-2500), the Princess Beach Hotel (599/961-4944), the Curaçao Caribbean Hotel (599/962-5000), the Golden Tulip Las Palmas (599/962-5400) are popular.

For music and dancing, try Naick's Place (599/96-14640).

The Willemstad Room at the Curaçao Caribbean has wonderful floor shows (599/962-5000).

For more information contact the Curaçao Tourist office at 400 Madison Ave., New York, NY 10017 or call 800/332-8266. On the island, the main tourist office is at Waterfront Plaza near the Curaçao Beach Hotel (599/961-3397).

TRINIDAD and TOBAGO

Take your choice: a lively island with a cosmopolitan capital that hosts one of the best annual parties in the world, or a quiet island oasis with uncrowded beaches, small villages, and natural wonders. That's what visitors to Trinidad and Tobago may choose from.

Trinidad is 50 miles long by 37 miles, almost 16 times the size of Tobago (26 miles by 7), its sister island 22 miles away.

Trinidad is famous as the home of Carnival, the lusty, lavish, bacchanal held every year in late February or early March. The prelenten festival is celebrated on many other islands in the Caribbean. The Carnival in Port-of-Spain, capital of Trinidad, is by far the biggest and the best.

The celebration is primarily one of music and extravagant costumes. The music begins several nights before "Mas Tuesday," with steel bands and calypso singers competing at the Queen's Park Racetrack. After the coronation of the Calypso Monarch, king of the festival, the festivities spill into the streets of the town, continuing until midnight of Fat Tuesday.

It's more fun than Mardi Gras, mainly because in Trinidad there is more stress on music and fun than there is in drinking one's self into oblivion as in New Orleans.

The rest of the year, the capital of 1.2 million residents is the shopping, business, industrial, and cultural center of the island. The best sights in town are the colonial and gingerbread homes along Pembroke Street and the Savannah, officially known as Queen's Park. The park is home to the racetrack, numerous grand old homes, and the Royal Botanic Gardens, with more than 700 species of orchids.

For sunworshippers, all the beaches are outside Port-of-Spain, with the prettiest, Blachisseuse Bay and Law Cuevas Bay, on the north coast road.

While driving to these beaches, take time to visit the Asa Wright Nature Center in the mountainous north. There you can see rare orange orchids, more than 100 exotic species of birds, and some beautiful vistas.

Exploring Tobago is very different than visiting Trinidad. On this island, there are scores of beaches and few towns larger than a village. Ferries leave twice a day between Port-of-Spain and Scarborough on Tobago.

The best beaches on Tobago are the northern shore. Try Store Bay, where you can catch a boat for a snorkeling trip to Bucco Reef, famous for its abundant marine life; Stone Haven Bay, where development has just started; or, for the most romantic spot, the pink sands of Lover's Bay to the north. The latter is reachable only by boat, but you can arrange passage on the waterfront there.

Romantic Retreats

Unfortunately, the nicest hotels on Trinidad are far from a beach. On Tobago, all are on or very near beaches.

The rates are for a room for two per night and do not include meals unless noted. The three categories are:

Inexpensive—Less than $100
Expensive—$100 to $200
Very expensive—$200 and more

Meal plans are offered at many hotels and can help cut costs. All-inclusive plans offer all meals, snacks, drinks, wine, entertainment, activities, sports, gratuities, and airport transfers for one fee, which ranges from $1,000 to $3,000 per person per week. Whether that is a bargain depends on how much you eat, drink, and play and whether you want more freedom to sample restaurants elsewhere on the island. Check your travel agent for current tariffs and the all-inclusive and other meal plans.

Our choices on Trinidad:

Asa Wright Nature Center. This park lodge offers 16 simple, but comfortable rooms in the center of the island's most beautiful region. The atmosphere is homey and guests share a living room and library.

Carnival

The annual island festival of Carnival is an extravagant celebration of colorful costumes, exciting island music and the drama of freedom, renewal, death, and destruction.

The Carnival parade fills the streets of the islands with towering Mocko Jumbis (stilt dancers) and Pitchy Patchies (figures in colorful patchwork costumes).

The celebrants dress in masks, costumes, and sequins symbolizing a dramatic theme—freedom, death, destruction, and renewal. Their goal is to be judged the most splendid costume at the Carnival.

"Carnival costumes are the ultimate symbols of liberation—the liberation of Everyman," says Geoffrey Holder, a Trinidad artist and choreographer.

The biggest and most gaudy Carnival is in Trinidad, where the festival began 200 years ago when French agricultural experts imported by Spanish colonists brought their pre-lenten Mardi Gras festival with them. The slaves donned their own costumes in response to mock their masters but started adding their own African influences to them.

Trinidad's Carnival takes place the Monday and Tuesday before Ash Wednesday, at the same time it takes place in St. Lucia and Dominica. The date of Carnival varies on other islands and some do not celebrate it at all. The schedule is as follows:

Anguilla—First weekend in August
Antigua—Late July and August
Aruba—Pre-lenten period
Bahamas—Dec. 26 and New Year's Day
Barbados—Mid-July to August
Bonaire—Pre-lenten period
Cayman Islands—April
Curaçao—Pre-lenten period
Dominica—Varies
Grenada—Mid-August
Guadeloupe—Ash Wednesday
Jamaica—Mid-April
Martinique—Pre-lenten period
Nevis—First Monday in August

St. Barts—Pre-lenten period
St. Kitts—Dec. 24–Jan. 2
St. Lucia—February
St. Maarten/St. Martin—Pre-lenten period
St. Vincent and Grenadines—Last week of June, early July
Trinidad & Tobago—Pre-lenten period
Turks & Caicos—Late August, early September
U.S. Virgin Islands—Last two weeks of April

Rates include all meals. (This place books up far ahead of time, so make your reservation six months ahead of your trip.) Inexpensive. 809/667-4655 or 800/426-7781.

Hotel Normandie. A grab-bag of architectural design and decor, this 61-room hotel offers nicely furnished rooms. Facilities include a pool. Inexpensive. 809/624-1181.

Trinidad Hilton. This large (442 rooms) luxury hotel is the capital's finest, offering first-class rooms, facilities, and prices. Attractions include pool, tennis courts, and a health club. Expensive. 809/624-3211.

On Tobago:

Arnos Vale Hotel. The 32 rooms in the white-stucco cottages at this hillside resort and former sugar plantation are just steps away from an uncrowded beach. Amenities include tennis courts and water sports. Expensive. 809/639-2881.

Mt. Irvine Bay Hotel. The beach is across the street at this 64-room (and 42-cottage) resort built on the ruins of a sugar plantation on 27 landscaped acres next to a golf course. The rooms offer exceptional views. Facilities include a pool, golf course, and tennis courts. Expensive. 809/639-8871.

Blue Waters Inn. Rustic, romantic, and beautiful, this 20-room inn offers a garden-like setting and uncrowded beaches. Facilities include tennis courts and dive school. Inexpensive. 809/661-4341.

For information about homes you can rent, please read the chapter "A Villa of Your Own."

Dining and Nightlife

The following price categories for restaurants are for dinner for two, without wine or alcoholic beverages:

Inexpensive—$30 and less
Moderate—$30 to $50
Expensive—$50 to $100

Our choices on Trinidad are all in Port-of-Spain:

La Boucan. Amid candlelight and piano music, formal waiters serve fine Creole and French dishes. What more can you ask? Expensive. 809/624-3211.

Café Savanna. Trinidadian dishes are served in casual surroundings. Expensive. 809/622-6441.

La Fantasie. The dining room is modern and lovely; the cuisine, Creole, Trinidadian, and a touch of French. Expensive. 809/624-1181.

On Tobago:

Old Donkey Cart House. Located in an Edwardian house near Scarborough, this excellent restaurant serves superb seafood dishes and a bit of fun. On Sunday evenings, the food may be accented with movies, slide shows, and live music. Moderate. 809/639-3551.

Sugar Mill. This elegant and romantic restaurant in the Mt. Irvine Bay Hotel is located in a renovated eighteenth-century mill. The fixed-price dinner, usually featuring seafood, is famous on the island. Moderate. 809/639-8871.

For nightlife in Trinidad, the hotel lounges are popular. If you want to get out of the hotel, try the Calypso Lounge at the Holiday

Inn (809/625-3361) and the Cricket Wicket (80-9/622-1808) for music and dancing. For native Calypso, head to Sparrow's Hideaway, about eight miles outside of Port-of-Spain. They don't have a phone, but all the taxi drivers know where it is.

On Tobago, almost all the entertainment is in the hotels. Check with them.

For more information contact the Trinidad and Tobago Tourist Board in the Forest Hills Tower, 118–35 Queens Blvd., Queens, NY 11375 or call 718/575-3909. On the islands, the Trinidad Tourist Board is at 122-24 Frederick St., Port-of-Spain (809/623-1932). On Tobago, the offices are in Scarborough Hall in Scarborough (809/639-2125).

The beach is long and uncrowded at the fabulous Cotton Bay resort on Eluthera in the Bahamas. (*Photo courtesy of Cheryl Andrews & Associates.*)

CHAPTER 5

The Bahamas and the Turks and Caicos

THE IMAGES THESE ISLANDS bring to mind are often misleading. Mention the Bahamas, and the image, carefully formed in commercials and advertisements, is of an island near Florida filled with casinos, Vegas-style nightclubs, and golf courses. Mention Turks and Caicos and many people will think of the Middle East; so a little refresher course is in order.

First, the Bahamas and the Turks and Caicos are not in the Caribbean. They are in the Atlantic Ocean.

Second, they are not three or four islands. The Bahamas are made up of more than 700 islands, most of them uninhabited. The northernmost islands are 50 miles east of Florida and curve south some 760 miles to the Turks and Caicos. The latter two island groups have only eight large islands and more than 40 small cays. Only six of the large islands and two of the cays are inhabited.

The Bahamas are known for casinos, nightclubs, and golf courses, but visitors will find few of those places on the Family Islands (or Out Islands), the distant and often less-developed sisters of the popular New Providence, Paradise, and Grand Bahamas islands. What visitors will find on those Family Islands are unspoiled beaches and elegant resorts.

Like the Family Islands, the Turks and Caicos have no glittering nightclubs and no casinos, just unspoiled beaches and some of the best diving in the world.

Taken as a whole, these two island groups, the Bahamas and the Turks and Caicos, offer dazzling nightlife, challenging golf, luxury resorts, quaint inns, exciting reefs, and long stretches of unspoiled, empty beaches.

THE BAHAMAS

The Bahamas present so many different faces that it is hard to sum them up in one paragraph. The major tourist islands are often identified only by the major city. Thus New Providence Island is also known as Nassau and Grand Bahama is known as Freeport/Lucaya. Paradise Island, a popular resort area, is just a bridge's length away from New Providence.

Nassau's major attractions include Fort Charlotte, the 200-year-old fortress overlooking the harbor, and Bay Street, the shopping haven for visitors.

Nature lovers will appreciate the 18-acre Botanical Gardens with 600 varieties of flowers, Coral World's underwater observatory on Silver Cay, and the Royal Victoria Gardens just off Shirley Street near Government House.

Paradise Island is the large hotel district, though the bridge to it goes over Potters Cay, where islanders sell fruit and vegetables and shell their conch catches.

The sights on Freeport include the Arts and Crafts Market, the Straw Market, and the International Bazaar, the latter two reached through the Japanese Torii gate next to the Princess Resort.

(Before you plunge heavily on the luxury items in the shops, you should know that the Bahamas are not a duty-free territory. While you may find some luxury items with prices lower than those in the states, the majority of the prices are no bargain. The prices of crafts, artworks, and other locally made items are bargains.)

Freeport is also the site of the Grand Bahama Museum, which displays artifacts of the Lucayana Indians who inhabited the islands where Columbus discovered them.

Natural wonders abound in the Lucayan National Park: a 40-acre wonderland of exotic tropical flora; the Rand Memorial Nature Center, a 100-acre park with hundreds of different plants and more than 200 species of birds; and the Perfume Factory on Eight Mile Rock, where local flowers are made into fragrances.

On the Out Islands, there are few attractions on land other than pristine, empty beaches, colorful villages, and a few historic buildings.

On Green Turtle Cay in the Abacos, the village of New Plymouth resembles a Cape Cod town, albeit for the tropical vegetation. The Albert Lowe Museum in the village displays artifacts and other items going back to the first settlers.

Andros, the largest of the Bahamas islands at 110 miles long and 40 miles wide, has a great barrier reef off its eastern coast. It's the third largest reef in the world and has some spectacular coral and marine life. The reef leads to the Wall, a sheer dropoff to the 6,000-foot-deep region known as the Tongue of the Ocean.

Andros is also known for its Blue Holes, the more than 200 huge round holes in the limestone floor of the ocean, and the Androsia Batik Works in Fresh Creek.

The main attractions on Cat Island are the Hermitage, a gray stone abondoned abbey, and the ruins of two colonial estates, Deveaux Plantation and Armbister Plantation.

Eluthera is a long (110 miles), thin (5 miles at most) island that is the most beautiful of the Bahamas. The major attractions include the Ocean Hole—the odd round cavern entrance on the seafloor at Tarpoum Bay, the Gregory Town and Hatcher Bay plantations, and the historic old churches of Harbour Island.

Exuma, a chain of more than 350 tiny islands bisected by the Tropic of Cancer, is popular for its fishing, shells, and diving.

San Salvador, once believed to be where Columbus first landed in the New World, is the home of the New World Museum of the Sea.

Romantic Retreats

The rates are for a room for two per night and do not include meals unless noted. The three categories:

Inexpensive—Less than $100
Expensive—$100 to $200
Very expensive—$200 and more

Meal plans are offered at many hotels and can help cut costs. All-inclusive plans offer all meals, snacks, drinks, wine, entertainment, activities, sports, gratuities, and airport transfers for one fee, which ranges from $1,000 to $3,000 per person per week. Whether that is a bargain depends on how much you eat, drink, and play, and whether you want more freedom to sample restaurants elsewhere on the island. Check your travel agent for current tariffs and the all-inclusive and other meal plans.

On the smaller Out Islands, take the meal plan. Your options to dine outside the resort are usually very limited, if nonexistent.

Our choices on Nassau/New Providence:

Coral World Villas. One end of the suite faces the sea and the other a private pool in this small (22 beautiful suites) hotel near the Coral World Undersea Laboratory. Expensive. 809/328-1036 or 800/221-0203.

Graycliff Hotel. Perhaps the finest inn listed in this book, the 12 rooms in this historic mansion are magnificent. Facilities include a pool, gym, solarium, and five-star restaurant. Expensive. 809/322-2796.

Le Meridien Royal Bahamian. Luxury in style and service is the mark of this 170-room resort. The rooms, spacious and beautifully decorated, are either in the stately pink main house or in the pink villas on the grounds. Facilities include a beach, pool, tennis, fitness club, and spa. Expensive. 809/327-6400.

Nassau Beach Hotel. The 411 rooms in this luxury hotel are spacious and furnished tastefully with all the modern necessities. Amenities include a beach, pool, spa, tennis, and water sports. Very expensive. 809/327-7711 or 800/223-5672.

On Paradise Island:

Ocean Club. Once the home of Huntington Hartford, this 70-room luxury resort is filled with antiques and other fine furnishings.

Facilities include a beach, tennis courts, and water sports center. Very expensive. 809/363-2501 or 800/321-3000.

On Grand Bahama:

Lucayan Beach Resort & Casino. The 247 rooms are spacious and well-appointed in this resort on one of the island's better beaches. Amenities include tennis and water sports. Expensive. 809/373-7777.

Xanadu Beach & Marine Resort. This high-rise pyramid was famous as the hideaway of billionaire Howard Hughes. The 184 rooms are large and tastefully furnished. Amenities include a marina, golf, water sports, beach, and pool. Expensive. 809/352-6782 or 800/222-3788.

In the Abacos:

Abaco Inn. The 10 cottages are rustic at this quiet resort on Elbow Cay. Facilities include a pool and water sports center. Expensive. 809/367-2666.

Bluff House Club and Marina. The 25 rooms are large and well decorated in this ocean-front resort on Green Turtle Cay. Facilities include private beach, pool, and tennis courts. Expensive. 809/367-5211.

Green Turtle Club. The 30 rooms in this resort on Green Turtle Cay are large but not elegant. Facilities include a beach with a reef, dive shop, pool, and tennis courts. Expensive. 809/367-2572.

Small Hope Bay Lodge. This 20-cabin resort offers excellent though rustic accommodations and plenty of quiet. Facilities include a dive shop with instructions and a beach. Very expensive. 809/368-2014 or 800/223-6961.

On Eluthera:

Cotton Bay Club. The 75 rooms at this elegant resort are in small pink cottages. The decor is tropical and nice. Facilities include golf courses, tennis courts, pool, and beach. Very expensive. 809/334-2101 or 800/223-1588.

Winding Bay Beach Resort. There are 36 luxurious rooms in villas on this resort. Amenities include a beach, tennis, and water sports. Expensive. 809/334-2020 or 800/223-1588.

Pink Sands. The 46 comfortable, stone cottages on this resort on a pink beach make this a special place. Facilities include tennis courts. Expensive. 809/333-2030.

Runaway Hill. There are only eight rooms in this secluded inn, but all are comfortable. Pool and beach are available. Expensive. 809/333-2150 or 800/327-0787.

Windmere Island Club. The best accommodations in this 21-room resort are in the suites and villas. Unlike some resorts, they dress for dinner here. Amenities include two beaches, pool, and water sports. Very expensive. 809/322-2538 or 800/237-1236.

For information about homes you can rent, please read Chapter 10, "A Villa of Your Own."

Dining and Nightlife

We are listing restaurants only on the main three islands. On the Out Islands, the resorts we have listed also have the best dining rooms.

The following price categories for restaurants are for dinner for two, without wine or alcoholic beverages:

Inexpensive—$30 and less
Moderate—$30 to $50
Expensive—$50 to $100

In Nassau:

Europe Restaurant. Excellent American and Bahamian fare is served in an intimate atmosphere. Moderate. 809/322-8032.

Frilsham House. This restored mansion now serves some stun-

"At ten at night the Admiral, being in the sterncastle, saw light . . . like a small wax candle. The admiral was certain they were near land."

—Columbus' log

The 500th anniversary of the history-making voyage of Christopher Columbus is approaching, and several islands in the Bahamas and Caribbean are making plans to celebrate the event in 1992 and 1993.

Because festivals and anniversary celebrations attract tourists, just where *Columbus first landed in the New World could be big bucks for the lucky island.*

Columbus named that island San Salvador and noted that the Indians living their called it Guanahaní. But for two centuries, historians and naval experts trying to retrace the voyage have named nine different islands as the first landing spot.

All the sites are in the Bahamas. From northwest to southeast, they are: Egg Island, Cat Island, Conception Island, Watling Island, Samana Cay, Plana Cays, Mayaguana Island, East Caicos, and Grand Turk.

In 1986, the National Geographic *used Columbus' log and a computer to project wind, current, and sailing speed; the conclusion, Samana Cay. A subsequent field expedition discovered additional confirmation: evidence of Indian settlements, which Columbus had noted in the log.*

Samana Cay may not profit from its new-found celebrity as the famed landing site of the Admiral. Despite the discovery by Europeans almost 500 years ago, the island remains uninhabited.

ning continental and Hamania dishes in a very elegant setting. Expensive. 809/327-7639.

Graycliff. The continental and Bahamian dishes compete with the elegant, antique-filled setting in this wonderful inn. Expensive. 809/322-2796.

The Regency. Candlelight dining on a classic French menu is a delight in this restaurant in the Crystal Palace Resort. Expensive. 809/327-6000.

Sun And . . . . Fine French and Bahamian seafood is served in an elegant mansion. Expensive. 809/323-1205.

On Paradise Island:

Cafe Martinique. French cuisine, candlelight, and music make this spot, next to a lagoon, a very romantic dining room. Expensive. 809/326-3000.

The Courtyard Terrace. An elegant setting complements the superb continental and Bahamian dishes. Expensive. 809/325-7501.

On Grand Bahama:

Cafe Valencia. This casual popular spot serves up some creative Bahamian and Spanish dishes. Expensive. 809/352-8717.

Escoffier Room. The beautiful room can't compare to the excellent Bahamian dishes. Expensive. 809/352-6782.

For nightlife in Nassau and Paradise Island, try the casino in the Crystal Palace Hotel or the casino and Las Vegas-style shows in the Paradise Island Cabaret Theatre in the Paradise Island Hotel.

On Grand Bahama, the hotel nightclubs and the casinos in the Bahamas Princess and the Lucayan Beach Hotel are popular.

On the Out Islands, the resorts we listed have entertainment either nightly or several times during the week.

For more information contact the Bahamas Office of Tourism at 10 Columbus Circle, Suite 1660, New York, NY 10019 (212/758-2777), or write the Ministry of Tourism at P.O. Box N-3701, Nassau, The Bahamas.

THE TURKS AND CAICOS

These two island groups form an isolated British Crown Colony boasting few attractions other than beautiful beaches and outstanding reefs that attract divers from around the world.

The on-land attractions are few. There are no major towns, no busy duty-free shopping districts, and no majestic historic buildings. The sights worth visiting are the Conch Bar Caves, on Middle Caicos, the largest of the islands. There you can see underground lakes and some odd stalactite and stalagmite formations. On nearby North Caicos is the Flamingo Pond, the nesting site for the beautiful and odd birds.

After you visit those sites, it's time to put on your swimsuit and head to the beaches. There are no "best" beaches, but almost every island has long stretches of clean, almost empty shoreline.

Offshore, however, is another story. The major undersea attractions include Grand Turk's Wall, a sheer drop that reaches depths of 7,000 feet. On the Wall's face are exotic gardens of coral, caves, and countless forms of marine life.

The south end of South Caicos is popular for its shallower drop-off, and the staghorn and elkhorn coral on the east side draws snorkelers. Most of the beaches on North Caicos have reefs that are perfect for snorkeling. West Caicos' Northwest Reef has amazing fields of coral, but the currents can be dangerous. Only experienced divers should try it.

Romantic Retreats

The rates are for a room for two per night and do not include meals unless noted. The three categories:

Inexpensive — Less than $75
Expensive — $75 to $100
Very expensive — $100 and more

Meal plans are offered at many hotels and can help cut costs. All-inclusive plans offer all meals, snacks, drinks, wine, entertainment, activities, sports, gratuities, and airport transfers for one fee, which ranges from $1,000 to $3,000 per person per week. Whether that is a bargain depends on how much you eat, drink, and play and whether you want more freedom to sample restaurants elsewhere on the island. Check your travel agent for current tariffs and the all-inclusive and other meal plans.

On these islands, take the meal plan. There are few other restaurants available on many of the islands.

Our selections on Grand Turk:

Hotel Kittina. This resort has 54 modern beachfront rooms and simple but quaint accommodations in the nearby great house. Facilities include pool and dive shop. Very expensive. 809/946-2232 or 800/548-8462.

Island Reef. This beachfront hotel has 20 modern and comfortable rooms. Facilities include tennis courts and pool. Expensive. 809/946-2055 or 800/243-4954.

Salt Raker Inn. The accommodations here are not the most elegant on the island, but the 9 rooms and suites in this 150-year-old house have lots of charm. Expensive. 809/946-2260.

On Pine Cay:

The Meridian Club. This private 800-acre island has 15 rooms in cottages close to the unspoiled beach. Island facilities include a nature preserve, hiking trails, pool, tennis courts, and water sports center. Very expensive. 800/225-4255.

On Providenciales:

Erebus Inn. Located on a bluff offering spectacular views, this 30-room resort offers spacious and modern accommodations. Facilities include tennis courts, miniature golf course, and two pools. Very expensive. 809/946-4240.

Third Turtle Inn. One of the island's oldest inns and most popular hangouts, the hotel offers 15 large and comfortably furnished rooms. Facilities include tennis courts and marine and dive shop. Very expensive. 809/946-4230 or 800/223-7600.

On North Caicos:

Prospect of Whitby Hotel. The 28 rooms in this isolated hotel are comfortable. Facilities include dive shop and pool. Very expensive. 809/946-4250 or 800/346-4295.

Dining and Nightlife

Only two of the islands, Grand Turk and Providenciales, have restaurants worth noting.

The following price categories for restaurants are for dinner for two, without wine or alcoholic beverages:

Inexpensive — $30 and less
Moderate — $30 to $50
Expensive — $50 to $100
Very expensive — More than $100

On Grand Turk:

Island Reef. Local seafood is offered here along with some old Texas (!) favorites. Expensive. 809/946-2055.

Papillon's Rendezvous. French cuisine, more or less, is served with an emphasis on local seafood. Expensive. 809/946-2088.

Sandpiper. Candlelight dining is offered on a beautiful garden terrace. The menu features a mixture of continental and downhome dishes. Moderate. 809/946-2232.

On Providenciales:

Island Princess. Cute dining room and stunning views only add to the great seafood served here. Expensive. 809/946-4260.

Doras. This casual and charming dining room serves some excellent local seafood dishes. Inexpensive. (No phone.)

For nightlife, other than swapping diving lies, try the Uprising (no phone) on Grand Turk and the Banana Boat (809/946-4312) on Providenciales.

For more information contact the Turks and Caicos Tourist Board, c/o Medhurst & Associates, 271 Main St., Northport, NY 11768 or call 516/261-7474 and 212/936-0050. On Grand Turk, the tourist offices are on Front Street in Cockburn Town (809/946-2321).

Windsurfing is a popular sport in the waters off Bermuda. (*Photo courtesy of Bermuda Department of Commerce.*)

CHAPTER 6

Bermuda

BERMUDA IS A vibrant watercolor painting come to life. Pink beaches, turquoise waters, quaint homes, and cute cottages painted in pastels, the brilliant greens of the golf courses, and the everpresent gardens of flowers make Bermuda a very beautiful and romantic destination.

Located about 600 miles east of North Carolina's Outer Banks, there are seven large islands and more than 130 almost negligible islands in Bermuda. The seven large islands, the Bermuda that visitors know, are connected by bridges, creating a fishhook-shaped land-chain about 23 miles from tip to tip and no more than a half-mile wide at most.

On Bermuda are beautiful beaches, villages, and harbor towns anchored by some stunning examples of colonial and Georgian architecture, beautiful gardens, eerie caves, and magnificent large resorts. The islands surround five large sounds that offer clear water and reefs perfect for boating, scuba diving, snorkeling, and other water sports.

The season on this Atlantic resort is different from those in the Bahamas or Caribbean. The high season is May to October, when temperatures average in the mid to high 70s. The rest of the year, temperatures are in the 60s and low-70s.

Bermuda is divided into nine parishes, each of equal size but not equal attractions. In Sandys Parish, the western-most district, you can browse through the pottery, toys, and paintings at the Craft Market; see the exhibits at the Bermuda Arts Centre; or take an undersea tour on the submarine *Enterprise*. All three attractions are located on the Dockyard on Ireland Island.

Heading back toward the eastern end of Bermuda, you come across Southampton, Warwick, and Paget parishes. All are popular locations for homes, resort developments, and beachfront hotels. The Botanical Gardens in Point Finger Road in Paget Parish have 36 acres of beautiful and rare plants, including scores of types of the hibiscus blossoms.

Pembroke's main attraction is Hamilton, the capital and the only urbanized area on the island. Hamilton is small enough to tour on foot, but first, stop by the Visitors Service Bureau, on the west end of the cruiseship docks, and pick up maps of the city's sights and shops.

Front Street, the main boulevard facing the cruise-ship docks, is a colorful avenue of lively nightspots, restaurants, and shops. The City Hall on Church Street is also the home of the Society of Arts, where concerts are held in a theater and art exhibits are displayed in the gallery. The Par-La-Ville Gardens between Queen and Par-La-Ville streets, has offered a quiet place to stop for a rest since the mid-1800s.

The adjacent parishes—Devonshire and Smith's—are quiet, with little commercial development. Smith's, though, does present some striking views of Harrington's Sound from the road of the same name.

Hamilton Parish, on the other side of the sound, offers several natural wonders. In Bailey's Bay, the Crystal Caves hold a subterranean lake and abundant stalactites and stalagmites. The Amber Caves offer fantastic, amber-tinted underground formations; while the Bermuda Aquarium, Museum, and Zoo on the Sound Road display a variety of animals and marine life. Finally, the aroma from fragrant flowers and plants used to make perfume is enhanced at the Bermuda Perfumery and Gardens in Bailey's Bay. Tour guides will show you how the flowers in the gardens are used to make perfume at the small factory.

The eastern-most parish is St. George's, the capital of Bermuda for the British Crown Colony's first two centuries and still very much like it was in those days. On its small waterfront is King's Square, where the Visitor's Service Bureau offers maps, brochures, and other information on sights. Two popular attractions are the Stocks and Pillory, re-creations of the real ones used to punish miscreants centuries ago.

Also on the square are the Town Hall, built in 1782; the State House, where parliament met; and Bridge House, home of Bermudan governors and the notorious privateer Bridger Goodrich. Bridge House today displays and sells fine art and other gift items.

The streets leading away from the square are lined with shops and galleries selling fine crystal, clothing, and art. The buildings in this small town are low-rise, colorful, and usually graced by attractive and lush bushes, trees, and flowers.

On Bermuda's beaches you have something usually missing from the sands of the Caribbean, waves. Unlike the placid sea to the south, the Atlantic produces respectable waves, which become a bit tamed after passing over Bermuda's many reefs.

The best of the beaches are on the south and western shores. There you will find Somerset Long Bay, the curved Horseshoe Bay, the smaller beaches of Peel and Stonehole bays, and the long shore at Warwick Long Bay. Elbow Beach, famous for its superb resort as well as its pink sand beach, allows guests not staying at the hotel, for a small fee.

Getting around to see these and other sights is best done by a taxi tour guide. The cabs carry blue flags, indicating that the driver is a guide. You cannot rent a car on the island, although the adventurous may rent bicycles and mopeds (the small motorized cycles that are very popular with younger tourists).

Before you leave Bermuda, head over to the No. 1 Passenger Terminal on Front Street. There, you may hire a horse-drawn carriage, the perfect romantic ending to a day on this island paradise.

Romantic Retreats

Bermuda has numerous large luxurious resorts, all on or just a few minutes from a beach.

The rates are for a room for two per night and do not include meals unless noted. The three categories:

Inexpensive—Less than $100
Expensive—$100 to $200
Very expensive—$200 and more

Meal plans are offered at many hotels and can help cut costs. All-inclusive plans offer all meals, snacks, drinks, wine, entertainment, activities, sports, gratuities, and airport transfers for one fee, which ranges from $1,000 to $3,000 per person per week. Whether that is a bargain depends on how much you eat, drink, and play and whether you want more freedom to sample restaurants elsewhere on the island. Check your travel agent for current tariffs and the all-inclusive and other meal plans.

Our favorites:

Elbow Beach Hotel. Located on one of the island's most beautiful pink beaches, this elegant resort has 298 rooms in the main hotel, in cottages, or in villas closer to the water. Get a room in the villas or cottages, if you want serenity. Amenities include water sports, health club, pool, and tennis courts. Expensive. 809/236-3535 or 800/223-7434.

Glencoe Harbour Club. Small and popular with water-sports enthusiasts, this 41-room hotel is located in a 200-year-old waterfront building. The rooms are spacious and colorfully decorated. Some of the suites have fireplaces, jacuzzis, and balconies. Very expensive. 809/236-5274 or 800/468-1500.

Horizons and Cottages. This 50-room Paget resort offers a magnificent view of the Atlantic, marvelous rooms in a classic Bermudan resort, a private beach, golf courses, tennis courts, and a pool. Very expensive. 809/236-0048.

Lanata Colony Club. The 65 private cottages at this lovely resort overlooking the Great Sound are spacious (some are split-level suites) and beautifully decorated. Facilities include a pool, a garden-like setting, tennis courts, a tiny beach, and water sports center. Very expensive. 809/234-0141 or 800/468-3733.

Marriott's Castle Harbour Resort. This 415-room luxury hotel sits on a bluff offering a commanding view of Castle Harbour and Harrington Sound. The 250 acres of beautifully landscaped grounds contain a Robert Trent Jones golf course, tennis courts, three pools, and two gorgeous beaches. The guest rooms are spacious and furnished with antique reproductions. Other features are a water sports center and nightclub. Very expensive. 809/293-2040 or 800/228-9290.

Newstead. This harborside, antique-filled hotel offers 50 spacious and beautifully decorated rooms in the main house and in nearby cottages. Amenities include afternoon tea, beach club privileges, tennis courts, pool, and sauna. Expensive. 809/236-6060 or 800/468-4111.

Pink Beach Club. Named for its two pink beaches, this attractive and homey hotel has 72 rooms in cottages located in or near the extensive gardens. Facilities include a pool and tennis courts. Offshore, tropical fish can be spotted in the waters and along the reef. Very expensive. 809/293-1666 or 800/372-1323.

The Princess. Pink, pretty, and luxurious, this nineteenth-century landmark just outside Hamilton has attracted such notables as Mark Twain and Prince Charles. The lobby and public areas are a stunning blend of marble, fountains, waterfalls, and greenery—a magnificent setting. The 456 rooms are spacious and many have balconies. Amenities include two pools, beach club, and golf privileges. Expensive. 809/295-3000 or 800/223-1818.

The Reefs. Overlooking a private south-shore beach, this casual, secluded cliffside hotel has 60 comfortable lanai or cabana-style rooms. Features include pool and tennis. Expensive. 809/238-0222 or 800/223-1363.

Southampton Princess. This hilltop luxury hotel has 600 spacious rooms, most with stunning views and exchange privileges with the Princess Hotel just outside Hamilton. Facilities include a golf course, tennis courts, two pools, and transportation to a private beach club. Very expensive. 809/238-8000 or 800/268-7176.

Stonington Beach Hotel. The furnishings are beautiful at this 64-room hotel on a secluded south-shore beach. Facilities include a pool and tennis courts. Expensive. 809/236-5416 or 800/223-1588.

For information about homes you can rent, please read Chapter 10, "A Villa of Your Own."

Dining and Nightlife

The best food on Bermuda is the fresh seafood featured at most restaurants. Dining is very expensive and a 15 percent gratuity is automatically added to the bill. Reservations and jackets for men are required at most places.

The following price categories for restaurants are for dinner for two, without wine or alcoholic beverages:

Inexpensive—$50 and less
Moderate—$50 to $100
Expensive—More than $100

Our favorites:

Chez Lafitte. When you tire of continental and seafood entrees, head to this casual restaurant in Hamilton and dine on Creole, Cajun, African, Spanish, and other exotic dishes. Expensive. (No phone.)

Fourways Inn. Famous beyond Bermuda, this Paget restaurant serves stunning French and Bermudian dishes in a 263-year-old home. The fountain courtyard is very romantic. Expensive. 809/236-6517.

Lanatana Colony Club. This Sandys Parish restaurant offers a superb continental menu served in a room and terrace decorated with beautiful furniture, plants, flowers, and works of art. Dancing is offered on Tuesdays, Thursdays, and Saturdays. Expensive. 809/234-0141.

Margaret Rose. This dining room at the St. George's Club offers elegant candlelight dining and superb continental dishes. Moderate. 809/297-1200.

Newport Room. The setting in this elegant Southampton Princess restaurant is that of a luxurious, very posh club—dark wood, gleaming brass, silver, Wedgewood china, crystal—and the menu of nouvelle and Bermudian dishes complements the setting. Expensive. 809/238-8000.

New Harbourfront. Nouvelle cuisine, featuring pasta and seafood at this intimate waterfront restaurant in Hamilton across from the ferry dock. Expensive. 809/295-4207.

The Norwood Room. Elegant setting amid lots of greenery and a view of the water in the Stonington Beach Hotel, and creative continental dishes. Expensive. 809/236-5416.

Once Upon a Table. This beautifully decorated Victorian Home in Pembroke Parish serves up some of the finest continental fare on the island. Expensive. 809/295-8585.

Waterlot Inn. Dining on the terrace or in the historic tavern downstairs and the superb continental fare at this Southampton restaurant have attracted such notables as Mark Twain and James Thurber. Expensive. 809/238-0510.

For nightlife, the major hotels have floor shows, music, and dancing (sometimes during dinner) most nights. Stay at your own resort, or visit the biggest one nearby.

In Hamilton, the pubs of Front Street offer entertainment. The most popular are the Forty Thieves Club (809/292-4040), the Oasis Club (809/292-4978), and Rum Runners (809/292-4737).

For more information contact the Bermuda Department of Tourism at 310 Madison Ave., New York, NY 10017 or call 212/818-9800 and 800/223-6106. On the island, the tourist offices are at Global House, 43 Church St. in Hamilton (809/292-0023). The Visitors Service Bureaus are in the ferry landing on Front Street in Hamilton, on King's Square in St. George's, and at the airport.

Scuba diving is a popular sport on the reefs around Bermuda.

CHAPTER 7

Underwater Wonders

NOT ALL THE exotic sights on the islands are found on the beautiful sandy beaches, in the lush rain forests, on the slopes of the dormant volcanoes, or along the busy streets of the historic old port cities. Just offshore, visible even to non-swimmers, is a different world, an underwater one that is filled with myriad species of colorful marine life, majestic orchards of coral, and the wrecks of unlucky vessels.

The islands have underwater attractions for everyone. Non-swimmers may view the reef through the portholes of sightseeing submarines. Snorkelers have the choice of endless reefs and several underwater parks with marked trails, while experienced divers have several islands that are next to ocean "walls," where the seafloor suddenly plunges straight down for thousands of feet.

Almost every island has a dive school or agency offering diving and snorkeling lessons and cruises to the best of the underwater sights. Most hotel tours desks can fix you up with the adventure of your choice.

Here is the island-by-island rundown of where to dive and whom to call.

ANGUILLA

The waters off Mimi Bay, Sandy Hill, and Sandy Island (the last located about two miles offshore) are popular sites for snorkeling. Divers still search the waters off the eastern shore for relics from the wrecks of the Spanish galleons *El Buen Consejo* and *Jesus, María y José*, which sank in 1772.

Call Tamarind Water Sports (809/497-2020), Sandy Island Enterprises (809/497-6395), and Tropical Watersports (809/497-6666).

ANTIGUA

The reefs near Half Moon Bay and Five Islands on Antigua and Cocoa Point on Barbuda are popular with divers and snorkelers. English Harbour is off-limits to divers seeking relics from the numerous wrecks there, but guides can take you to other sunken ships.

Call Dive Antigua (809/462-0256), Aquanaut Dive Center (809/463-1024), or the dive shop at the Runaway Beach Club (809/462-1318).

ARUBA

Snorkelers and divers favor the waters off Palm Beach. The wreck of the *Antilla*, a German freighter, is a popular attraction.

Call De Palm Tours (297/8-24545) or Pelican Watersports (297/8-23600, exts. 511 and 329).

BAHAMAS

The more than 700 islands in this group have clear waters and seemingly endless reefs for snorkeling and diving. Divers enjoy seeking wrecks in the channel between New Providence and Paradise Island and Nassau Harbor. Sandy Cay is another popular reef diving and wreckage site.

In Nassau, call Bahama Divers (809/323-2644) and Underwater Tours (809/322-3285). In Freeport, call the Underwater Explorers Society (809/373-1244). In the Abacos, call Walker's Cay Dive Shop (800/327-3714—outside Florida; 800/432-2092—in Florida) and dive Abacos (809/367-2014). In Andros, call Undersea Adventures (305/763-2188 and 800/327-8150). On Eluthera, call the dive shop at the Winding Bay Beach Resort (809/344-2020).

BARBADOS

The waters off Southern Palms and Casuarina Cove on the south and the entire west coast of the island are popular with divers and snorkelers. The Atlantic Submarine offers reef sightseeing dives (809/436-8929) and the red-sailed Jolly Roger "pirate ship" makes daily cruises to Folkestone Underwater Park, off Holetown. The park has an underwater snorkeling trail on Dottin's Reef and glass-bottom boats for those who prefer to stay dry.

Divers will enjoy exploring some "blue holes" on the ocean floor and the wreck of the *Stavronikita*, a Greek freighter sunk in 125 feet of water.

Call Dive Barbados (809/432-7090), the dive school at the Coral Reef Club (809/432-0833), the Dive Shop Ltd. (809/426-9947), Dive Boat Safari in the Hilton (809/427-4350), Underwater Barbados (809/428-3504), and Willie's Watersports (809/424-0888, ext. 7429).

BERMUDA

The most popular beaches for snorkelers are Church Bay, West Whale Bay, and Warwick Long Bay. There are more than 350 wrecks on the many reefs surrounding the islands.

Call Hartley's Underwater Helmet Diving Cruises (809/292-4434 and 809/234-2861), which offers guided tours whereby the guide and the guided wear helmets connected to an air supply above water. The shallow-water dives are safe and the walking is easy to learn. South Side Scuba also offers reef and wreck dives (809/238-8122, ext. 3182). Looking Glass Cruises has the *Enterprise* submarine, which goes sightseeing to depths of 90 feet (809/236-8000).

BONAIRE

Some divers will swear that Bonaire has the best reef diving in the western hemisphere, second in the world only to the diving on Australia's Great Barrier Reef. The best diving and snorkeling sights are in the Bonaire Marine Park, which is easy to find for it runs almost the entire length of the island's west coast. Forty-four of the best dive sites are marked by moorings.

If your hotel doesn't have a dive school, call Peter Hughes Dive Bonaire (607/277-3484 and 800/367-3484), Bonaire Scuba Center (201/566-8866 or 800/526-2370), and the Habitat Dive Center (802/ 496-5067).

BRITISH VIRGIN ISLANDS

There are good snorkeling sites off almost every island. Divers enjoy visiting the wreck of the R.M.S. Rhone off Salt Island. The reefs around Anageda are said to have claimed some 500 ships. The Baths off Virgin Gorda are definitely worth seeing.

Call Dive B.V.I. (809/495-5513); Caribbean Images, which also has glass-bottom boats (809/495-2563); and Baskin in the Sun (809/ 494-2858).

CAYMAN ISLANDS

Snorkelers head to the coral ledge south of George Town on the west coast of Grand Cayman, where most of the reefs are included in a marine park. Off the north shore of Little Cayman is Bloody Bay Wall, a 6,000-foot cliff that sends divers into ecstasy.

Call Aqua Delights (809/947-4786), Bob Soto's (809/949-2022), Nick's Aqua Sports (809/949-8745) and, on Cayman Brac, Peter Hughes Dive Tiara (809/948-7553). The *Atlantis* submarine dives as deep as 150 feet along a reef (809/949-7700). If that isn't deep enough, try Research Submersibles, which can descend to 800 feet (809/949-8296).

CURAÇAO

Scuba divers and snorkelers will enjoy the Curaçao Underwater Park off the southern coast. There are more than 12 miles of reef and an underwater nature trail.

Call Peter Hughes Underwater Curaçao (599/961-6666), Piscadera Watersport (599/962-5000, ext. 177), Sun Dive (599/962-4888), and Dive Curaçao & Watersports (599/961-4944, ext. 20).

DOMINICA

The water and reefs off Scotts Head, Woodford Hill, Picard Beach, Soufriére Bay, and Anse Noire are popular with snorkelers and divers.

Call Dive Dominica (809/448-2188) for scuba tours and Dominica Tours (809/448-2638) for snorkeling.

DOMINICAN REPUBLIC

Puerto Plata and Luperón Beach are popular with snorkelers. Scuba divers enjoy La Caleta, miles of reefs and underwater caves.

Call Mundo Submarino (809/566-0344).

GRENADA

The reef off the island's west coast attracts both scuba divers and snorkelers, with the 594-foot-long *Bianca C.* lying in 100 feet of water. The sea bottom off Point Saline on the southern end of the island is loaded with wrecks.

Call Go Vacations (809/440-3670), HMC Diving Centre (809/444-4258), and Virgo Watersports (809/444-4410).

GUADELOUPE

Popular snorkeling areas include the waters off Caravelle Beach and Malendure Beach.

Call Nautilius Club (590/98-85-69) or Chez Guy (590/91-81-72). The Papyrus (590/90-92-98) offers glass-bottom cruises.

JAMAICA

There are numerous reefs off the north shore for snorkeling, and the waters off Negril are popular with scuba divers.

Call Blue Whale Divers (809/957-4438), Caribbean Amusement (809/954-2123), Paul Dadd's Fantasia Divers (809/974-2353), and See and Dive Jamaica (809/972-2162).

MARTINIQUE

The best diving spots are the waters off St. Pierre, Precheur, Ilet Ramier, and Anses-d'Arlets.

Call Bathy's Club (596/66-00-00), Caraibe Coltri Club (596/76-42-42), and Carib Scuba Club (596/78-08-08).

PUERTO RICO

Snorkelers and scuba divers head to Sun Bay, Seven Seas, and Boquerón Beach.

Call Parguera Divers Training Center (809/899-4171), Caribe Aquatic Adventures (809/721-0303, ext. 3447), Castillo Watersports (809/791-6195), Coral Head Divers (809/850-7208), and the Cueva Submarina Training Center (809/872-3903).

ST. BARTHÉLEMY

The best reefs for snorkeling are off Eden Roc and Marigot beaches.

Call La Marine (590/27-70-34), Club La Bulle (590/27-68-93), and Dive With Dan (590/27-64-78).

ST. EUSTATIUS

Scuba divers like the waters off Orange Town, which hides in its waters cannons, ruins of former waterfront buildings, and perhaps as many as 200 ships.

Call Surfside Statia (800/468-1708).

ST. KITTS AND NEVIS

On St. Kitts, snorkelers favor Dieppe Bay; and on Nevis, Newcastle Bay, and Pinney's beach and the waters around Fort Ashby, where ruins of Jamestown can be seen.

Call Kenneth's Dive Centre (809/465-2670) and Caribbean Watersports (809/465-8050) on St. Kitt's. On Nevis, call Montpelier Plantation (809/469-5462), and the Oualie Beach Club (809/469-5329).

ST. LUCIA

Anse Cochon and Jalousie Bay are popular with snorkelers, while Anse Chastanet is popular with scuba divers.

Call Scuba St. Lucia (809/454-7355), Marigot Bay Resort (809/453-4357), and the Anse Chastanet Dive Shop (809/454-7335).

ST. MAARTEN/ST. MARTIN

The waters off Little Bay Beach, Maho Bay, Pelican Key, and Oyster Pond are popular with snorkelers, while Proselyte Reef, Inlet Pinel, and Flat Island are havens for scuba divers.

Call Tradewinds Dive Center (599/5-22167), Little Bay Watersports (599/5-22333), Maho Watersports (599/5-44387), Ocean Explorers (599/5-45252), Watersports Unlimited (599/5-23434), and Red Ensign Watersports (599/5-22929).

ST. VINCENT AND THE GRENADINES

Numerous reefs make this group of islands a popular destination for snorkelers and scuba devotees. The reefs off Bequia and St. Vincent are favored by divers while snorkelers head to the small islands called Tobago Cays.

On St. Vincent, call Dive St. Vincent (809/457-4714) and Mariner's Watersports (809/457-4228). In the Grenadines, call Dive Bequia (809/458-3504), Dive Mustique (809/456-4777), and Sunsports (809/453-3577).

TRINIDAD AND TOBAGO

The best snorkeling and diving is on Tobago, with Buccoo Reef gathering the best praise. Also popular dive spots are Flying Reef on the western coast and Man of War Bay.

On Tobago, call Dive Tobago (809/639-2266) and Tobago Scuba (809/660-4327). On Trinidad, call Scuba Shop Ltd. (809/658-2183).

TURKS AND CAICOS

The island of North Caicos is a great place for diving and snorkeling while Grand Turk's famed 7,000-foot-deep Wall draws expert divers.

On Grand Turk, call Omega Divers (809/946-2232) and Blue Water Divers (809/946-2432). On Providenciales, call Wet Pleasures (809/946-4455) and Provo Turtle Divers (809/946-4232).

U.S. VIRGIN ISLANDS

The best diving and snorkeling is off Buck Island, an underwater national park. The snorkeling is good off Secret Harbour and Hull Bay on St. Thomas; Trunk Bay, which has marked underwater trails, Hawksnest Bay and Salt Pond Cay off St. John; and Tamarind Reef Beach and Isaac Bay off St. Croix.

Call Underwater Safaris (809/774-1350), Joe Vogel Diving Co. (809/775-7610), and the St. Thomas Diving Club (809/524-4746). On St. Croix, call Caribbean Sea Adventures (809/773-6011), Sea Shadows (809/778-3850), and Snorkeling Safari (809/773-0951). On St. John, call Cruz Bay Watersports (809/776-6234), Snuba (809/776-6922), and St. John Watersports (809/776-6256).

The Caribbean and the Bahamas are a graveyard of ships. The most popular islands for diving on wrecks and hunting other sunken treasure are as follows.

Bahamas. *Both Nassau harbor and the west end of Paradise Island have harvested their share of ships. More than 150 have sunk on the harbor, while the reef off Paradise Island has claimed more than 30 vessels. Coins and artifacts are still being recovered, but Bahamian law requires that you turn over all finds to the government.*

Barbados. *More than 100 vessels have sunk in Carlisle Bay.*

Bonaire. *Cannons and other wreckage from ships are visible in the shallow waters off the eastern point of the island.*

British Virgin Islands. *The coral atoll off Anegada has claimed more than 500 ships over the centuries, while the wreck of the R.M.S. Rhone off Salt Island is a diving favorite.*

The Caymans. *The wrecks of the Balboa and the Oro Verde off Grand Cayman are popular with divers, while a Spanish galleon was recently discovered off Little Cayman.*

Jamaica. *Pedro Shoals has claimed countless ships, with the most famous being the four galleons that sunk in 1679. Treasures from those ships were recently recovered.*

Puerto Rico. *The wrecks of more than 20 Spanish ships can be seen in the waters just off Morro Castle.*

St. Thomas. *The harbor of Charlotte Amalie is the graveyard of more than 100 ships. Wreckage can be spotted even today.*

The *Sea Goddess*, one of the most elegant cruise ships in the world. (*Photo courtesy of Cunard.*)

CHAPTER 8

Five Special Cruise Ships

CRUISING IS A WONDERFUL way to sample different islands within a short time, but we feel that most cruise ships are not romantic. The big ships are like floating convention hotels filled with hundreds of cramped cabins with separate single berth beds. The romance-dampeners don't end there. Your meal times are set, your dining partners are total strangers, and the organized activities are endless and often inane. There is another way to find romance on board.

There are three cruise lines that sail ships that are a distinct change from the floating hotels. On these stylish ships the cabins are larger, and the beds are usually a double if not queen-size. On these ships, passengers are pampered with fine food served at the time they prefer to dine and at tables with or without guests. There are no midnight buffets, no passenger talent nights, no scavenger hunts or costume contests. Water sports, port tours, nightly dancing, and perhaps a small casino are available, but you can just sun yourself on the deck if you wish.

There are two other cruise ships—majestic Tall Ships—that offer more rustic accommodations, a more casual atmosphere, and more activities.

On these five cruise lines you can find the setting to match your dream of romance.

Bon voyage!

Sea Goddess I

This 344-foot-long ship is often mistaken for some sultan's private yacht. That's not surprising for the *Sea Goddess* is famed for its elegant appointments, spacious accommodations, meticulous service, superb food, and exotic ports of call.

There are only 58 cabins on board this ship, all on the outside and all called suite-rooms. Each is equipped with a sitting area with a seven-foot sofa, chairs and table, and home entertainment center consisting of a remote-controlled color television, VCR (the ship carries a library of 300 movies), radio, and bar/refrigerator. If you really must stay in touch with the world, a direct-dial telephone is in the cabin.

The sleeping area is a spacious queen-size bed, with a large window offering a sea view, and a curtain that can be pulled to offer privacy from the rest of the suite/room. (If the suite/rooms are not spacious enough, two can be combined to make an enormous suite.)

The ship also offers a health spa, supervised by the Golden Door Spa of Escondido, California, a gym, sauna, masseuse, library, small casino, pool, and whirlpool.

All of these accommodations and facilities are superbly furnished, combining the best of classic elegance with high fashion.

All food, wine, and refreshments are included as part of the cruise tariff, but unlike most all-inclusive resorts and shops, the Sea Goddess is famed for the high quality of the cuisine and vintages.

What all this elegance combines to create is what the "Cunard Line," owners of the two Sea Goddesses, calls "The luxury of choosing." You can meet and share your cruise experiences with as many of your fellow passengers as you desire, or you may have as much privacy as you wish, even having your meals served in your cabin.

A journey on this very special ship is not for everyone. But if you enjoy being pampered in elegant surroundings, the *Sea Goddess I* may make your next cruise very, very romantic.

The *Sea Goddess I* cruises the Caribbean from mid-November through mid-April. Itineraries include stops in the Leeward and Windward islands. Twice a season, the ship sails up the Amazon between stops in the Caribbean. The cruise pace, at all times, is unhurried.

The ship also offers special theme cruises. The "Epicurean Delights" cruises include two dinners prepared by a chef chosen in a competition directed by the editors of *Food & Wine* magazine. The chef also conducts informal cooking classes.

On the Golden Door Spa cruise, 10 counselors and trainers from the resort will offer health and fitness counseling, personalized exercise programs, aerobics, massage, and beach workouts. There are other cruises featuring more organized activities and on-board lectures by scholars expert in the area you are cruising.

The cost varies, of course. Fares for the seven-day cruises range from $4,200 to $5,900 per person, depending on the time sailed and the itinerary chosen. The price includes all food, wine, snacks and refreshments, and round-trip airfare from 24 gateway cities.

Call 800/458-9000.

Windstar Sail Cruises

Our cruise aboard a Windstar ship was after Barbara insisted that our next trip be on a sailboat. So we booked a trip on the *Wind Star*, a magnificent, 440-foot-long, gleaming white, sailing ship whose four masts rise 204 feet above the sea.

The first time we saw the *Wind Star* was in the Sir Francis Drake Channel off Tortola in the British Virgin Islands. It caught our imagination then and more than lived up to our fantasies during our voyage on board.

Casual elegance is the best description of life aboard the three almost-identical Windstar ships (*Wind Star, Wind Spirit,* and *Wind Song*). The 74 outside cabins aboard are large, equipped with a queen-size bed, remote-controlled color television, VCR, direct-dial telephones, a small sitting area with desk, a large (by nautical standards) bathroom, and far more closet and cabinet space than even we over-packers needed. Other amenities include a minibar, stereo, a cable news channel, and daily movies on the television (the ship carries a library of 350 movies).

The decor of the cabins was elegant yet simple, combining beautiful wood with pleasantly colored fabrics to create an attractive and inviting environment.

These sailing ships are different from most for the sails are trimmed and set by computer-controlled hydraulics, a system that leaves the decks clear of endless piles of lines and ropes. The same computer also controls the heel—the tilt caused by the wind—of the deck, limiting it to no more than six degrees. Never did the deck lean so much that the women on board could not wear high heels.

Ship facilities include a nightclub, small casino, pool, sun deck, gymnasium, masseuse, library, and shops.

Passengers have the freedom to choose the type of cruise they want, from one of privacy to a journey that is more social. There are no set dining times nor table assignments. You can eat alone or with new-found friends; and best of all, the food is outstanding!

There are daily water sports and port tours, but the only scheduled ship-board activity is a nightly cocktail hour chat on the next day's port.

Like the *Sea Goddess,* the atmosphere is casual elegance. Although the nightclub and casino were available most nights for drinks and dancing, most passengers drifted to the open deck at the stern of the boat. There, we talked with other passengers, gazed out at the lights on the passing shoreline, and looked up at the huge white sails glowing brilliantly from floodlights.

The moment is magic, and you can share it.

Only two of the Windstar ships—the *Wind Star* and the *Wind Spirit*—cruise the Caribbean. During their November-to-April season, the itineraries include six-, seven-, and eight-day trips around the Leeward and Windward Islands.

Some voyages invite guest scholars to accompany the passengers and talk about the ports of call. Writer James Michener, for example, sailed on one *Wind Star* cruise in March, 1990, and talked about the Caribbean, the subject of his most recent book.

The cruise fares range from $1,595 to $2,895 per person, depending on the length of the voyage and the time of the cruise. Fares include all meals, but not drinks or wine. Air packages are available at extra cost.

Call 800/258-SAIL.

Renaissance Cruises

This new cruise line is operating five elegant ships (*Renaissance I–V*), all about 290-feet long and all boasting 50 to 57 superbly appointed suite/rooms, an atmosphere of casual elegance, and on-board experts who conduct seminars and slide shows on the art, culture, and history of the next port of call.

The suites are all outside with sea views and may be the most elegant available among the ships listed in this chapter.

The sleeping area, decorated in dark woods and elegant fabrics, has a queen-size bed, dresser, chairs, remote-controlled television and VCR, and telephone. The stylish sitting area, decorated in dark hardwood and gleaming brass, offers a sofa, chairs, cocktail table, and bar. The bathroom and closet storage space are also commodious.

The three categories of accommodations are the Renaissance Suites, located on the top deck with private balconies; the Deluxe Suites, on the three middle decks with three large windows; and the Superior Suites, on the lower deck with portholes.

The dining room is beautifully furnished and is able to seat all guests at one time; thus you can dine when and with whom you desire. The cuisine is international, but the emphasis is on healthier, lighter fare.

The ships also have a small club with piano bar, blackjack tables, pool, jacuzzi, sauna, water sports facilities, VCR tape library, and lounge.

The atmosphere is casual elegance, a bit less formal than aboard the *Sea Goddess I*; but the Renaissance vessels, merging the latest in technology and amenities while emphasizing the high standards of service of old, are wonderful ships in which to take a romantic cruise.

The five Renaissance cruise ships are the first of what will become an eight-ship line. *Renaissance I–IV* are 290-feet long with 50 cabins. *Renaissance V* is 297-feet long and has 57 cabins, as will the other three ships to be put into service by Spring, 1991.

Renaissance cruises include the Leewards, Netherlands Antilles, and Greater Antilles from November through mid-April. The cruises are 7-, 10-, and 14-days long. Fares range from $2,330 to $5,615 depending on the type of accommodations, the time sailed, and the length of the cruise. The prices include all food, snacks, and round-trip air fare, but not wines and liquor.

Call 305/463-0985.

Windjammers

Less elegant than the ships mentioned earlier, a cruise aboard these six majestic Tall Ships in the Windjammer Barefoot Cruise fleet is relaxed and filled with fun.

The six ships are beautiful vessels ranging in size from 197 feet to 282 feet. Here is a description of the ships:

Amazing Grace, a 243-foot former British Navy ship which has hosted Queen Elizabeth, is the newest Windjammer. It can hold 100 passengers during its 19-day voyage from the Bahamas around the Caribbean. The ship serves as a supply ship for the fleet and thus meets with every Windjammer during the voyage.

Fantome is the largest ship in the fleet at 282 feet. Built for the Duke of Westminster and later bought by Aristotle Onassis as a wedding gift for Prince Ranier and Princess Grace of Monaco, this majestic ship holds 126 passengers. It makes six-day voyages out of Port-of-Spain and Trinidad, stopping on the island of Tobago four times.

Flying Cloud, a 208-foot-long former training ship for the French navy, can host 74 passengers during its seven-day sails in the British Virgin Islands.

Mandalay is famous for the American Express commercial in which a couple struggling to sail a small boat decides to abandon ship and sign on as passengers on an extraordinary Tall Ship that appears out of nowhere. The Mandalay, a 236-foot-yacht once owned by E.F. Hutton, is that ship. It can carry 72 passengers on 13-day voyages out of Antigua and Grenada.

Polynesia is a 248-foot Portuguese Bank schooner which carries 126 passengers on week-long sails in the Leeward and Windward Islands.

The Yankee Clipper, a 197-foot yacht originally built in 1927 for German arms baron Alfred Krupp, carries 66 passengers on week-long cruises of the Leewards.

The key to a successful romantic voyage on these vessels is the choice of accommodations. The Admiral Suites are best for they offer more room, more storage space, and a double bed. These cabins are on the main deck. The cabins below deck are smaller, and the beds may be side-by-side single bunks. All the cabins are rustic, but have private baths, electricity, and air conditioning.

The meals on board are bountiful and good, but not haute cuisine. Dining is informal, and the lunch is usually a buffet or beach picnic.

The ships offer myriad activities from joining in the trimming of the sails to fishing, sailing classes, port tours, and limbo contests. There is no pressure to join in the activities, though.

For couples seeking a more casual and activity-filled cruise, the Windjammer fleet may be the ships of choice.

Cruise-only rates for six-day voyages aboard the *Flying Cloud, Yankee Clipper*, and *Polynesia* range from $675 to $850 per person.

Rates for the *Mandalay*'s 13-day voyage are $1,350 to $1,550 per person; rates for the *Amazing Grace* and its 19-day voyage are $1,275 to $1,500; and fares for the *Fantome* and its six-day cruise around Tobago are $600 per person.

The rates include food and drink but not air fare. Air packages are available.

Call 800/327-2601; in Florida, call 305/672-6453.

Tall Ship Adventures

The *Sir Francis Drake*, a 162-foot three-masted Tall Ship built in 1917 in Germany, sails the Virgin Islands offering its small group of passengers a relaxed cruise with few activities, no fixed itinerary, and superb food.

There are 15 cabins on this ship, all with private baths, air conditioning, tasteful wood panelling, and carpeting. The best cabins are the six with double beds.

The food on board is surprisingly good considering the size of the ship. Jamaican chef Newton Hood serves up some marvelous creations drawing on the fine dishes of the West Indies.

Activities include daily snorkeling and scuba trips and tours of island resorts and ports.

Most of all, the *Sir Francis Drake* provides a peaceful platform from which to savor the serenity of the sea and sun.

The *Sir Francis Drake* makes three-, four-, and seven-day cruises year-round in the U.S. and British Virgin Islands. Rates range from about $450, $575, and $900 respectively. Other air and combination sea/land packages are available.

Call 800/662-0090.

The harbor on Charlotte Amalie in St. Thomas is popular with sailors. (*Photo courtesy of U.S. Virgin Islands Division of Tourism.*)

CHAPTER 9

Be Your Own Captain

THE SHORELINES OF THE romantic islands are often cluttered by the presence and creations of man. Hotels, boat docks, warehouses, and homes are intrusions that spoil the green landscape beyond the sands.

From the sea, however, these man-made creations shrink, dwindling in size as the ship you are aboard sails out into the blue waters. From a mile out, even the large resorts seem almost miniscule. From two miles out to sea, only the tallest buildings are visible.

From a sailboat or motor yacht, the natural beauty of these islands takes hold. Mountain landscapes linger on the horizon, promising adventure and new experiences.

We have sailed in the Caribbean and Atlantic during our visits to these islands, and the experience is so captivating that we still dream of one day chartering a large sailboat—perhaps a 50′ to 60′

sloop—and hiring a captain to sail us around the British Virgin Islands, the Family Islands in the Bahamas, or just around St. Lucia and the other Windward isles.

On your own boat you can chart your own course. If the bay you are in is stunning, stay! If the port offers some fine shops and restaurants, stay! The choice is yours, for the ship is yours.

The cost of living this fantasy is fairly reasonable and depends mainly on the size of the boat. A 50-foot sailboat with crew can be chartered for about $3,000, everything included, for a week during the high season. The price goes up with the size of the ship. Power boats are more expensive.

Living on a ship requires some accommodations. The cabins are not spacious, the baths (called "heads") at best will have a hand-held shower, and the closeness may test the compatibility of a couple. There is no place to go to be alone, except on land.

What you get with your own ship is the power to choose where you wish to sail, when and where you wish to anchor and take a swim or snorkel, what ports to visit, and when you want to go ashore.

Finally, if the cabins seem to be getting smaller, and the shower never seems to leave you feeling clean, ask the captain to head to one of the many inns, resorts, or hotels with marinas and spend a night onshore.

If the thought of a week on board is a bit intimidating, try taking a day sail or even a sunset cruise. Even on these shorter voyages, the islands will seem like lush jewels from the surface of the ceaseless seas.

Chartering a Boat

There are scores of yacht brokers that can arrange a ship and crew to meet your needs. You will be asked whether you want a "bareboat" charter or a "crewed" charter. Bareboat means you get nothing but the boat, no food, no crew, nothing. You stock and sail the ship yourself. The chartering agency will require proof that you are capable of sailing the yacht. "Crewed" boats are usually stocked with food and carry a captain and cook and other crew as needed.

Here is a listing of the yacht brokers:

Bahamas Yachting Services, 2 Prospect Park, 3347 NW 55 St., Ft. Lauderdale, FL 33309 (800/327-2276). Crewed and bareboat, and sailing classes.

Bimini Yacht Charters, 1051 Clinton St., Buffalo, NY 14206 (716/855-2774). Crewed and bareboat.

Blue Water Cruises, P.O. Box 758, St. Thomas, USVI 00801. 800/524-2020 (Crewed).

Boat U.S. Travel, 800 South Pickett St., Alexandria, VA 22304 (800/BOAT USA and 703/751-6456). Crewed and bareboat.

Caribbean Sailing Yachts, Box 491, Tenafly, NY 07670 (800/631-1593). Bareboats, with or without skipper.

Caribbean Yacht Charters, P.O. Box 583, Marblehead, MA 01945 (800/225-2520). Bareboats, skippers on request.

Endless Summer Charters, Sanctuary Centre, Suite 306A, 4800 N. Federal Highway, Boca Raton, FL 33431 (800/843-5747). Crewed.

The Moorings Ltd, 1305 U.S. 19 South, Suite 402, Clearwater, FL 34624 (813/535-1446). Crewed or bareboats.

Nicholson Yacht Charters, 9 Chauncy St., No. 50, Cambridge, MA 02138 (800/662-6066). Luxury boats with crews.

North-East Wind Yacht Charter, P.O. Box 4220, 326 First St., Annapolis, MD 21403 (800/638-5139 and 301/267-6333). Bareboats.

Ocean Escapes, P.O. Box 6009, Newburyport, MA 01950 (800/227-8633). Crewed and barefoot.

Regency Yacht Vacations, P.O. Box 9997, St. Thomas, USVI 00801 (800/524-7676). Crewed and bareboat.

Virgin Island Sailing Ltd, P.O. Box 4065, St. Thomas, USVI 00801 (800/648-3393, 800/233-7936 and 809/494-2774). Crewed and bareboat.

Yacht Vacations, P.O. Box 11179, St. Thomas, USVI (800/524-5008). Crewed.

Day Cruises

For day sails, snorkeling cruises and even sunset cruises, contact these companies if your hotel's tour desk cannot find you a boat:

Anguilla

Sandy Island Enterprise—809/497-6395.
Tamariand Water Sports—809/497-2020.

Antigua

The Falcon—809/462-4792.
Paradise I—809/462-4158.
Wadadli Watersports—809/462-4101.

Aruba

De Palm Tours—297/8-24545.
Pelican Watersports—297/8-23600.

Bahamas

Bayshore Marina—809/326-8232.
Nassau Yacht Haven—809/322-8173

Barbados

Jolly Roger Watersports—809/426-0767.
Captain Patch Cruises—809/427-2525.
Barbados Cruising Club—809/426-4434.

Bermuda

Bermuda Water Sports—809/293-2640.
Bermuda Water Tours—809/295-3727.
Bermuda Yacht Charters—809/293-2040.
Sail Bermuda—809/238-0774.

Bonaire

Habitat Dive Center—809/496-5067.
Bonaire Scuba Center—800/526-2370.
Peter Hughes Dive Bonaire—800/367-3484.

British Virgin Islands

Bitter End Yacht Club—809/494-2746.
B.V.I. Bareboats—809/494-4289.
Go Vacations—809/495-2374.
The Moorings Ltd—809/494-2331.

Cayman Islands

Aqua Delights—809/947-4786.
Bob Soto's—809/949-2022.
Don Foster's—809/949-7025.

Curaçao

Peter Hughes Underwater Curaçao—599/961-6666.
Piscadera Watersports—599/962-5000, ext. 177.

Dominica

Dominica Tours—809/448-2638.

Dominican Republic

Heavens—809/586-5250.
Casa de Campo—809/682-2111 or 800/223-6620.

Grenada

Go Vacations—809/440-3670.

Guadeloupe

Evasion Marine—590/84-46-67.
Papyrus—590/90-92-98.

Jamaica

Blue Whale Divers—809/957-4438.
Caribbean Amusement—809/954-2123.

Martinique

Affaires Maritimes—596-71-90-05.
Club de la Voile de Fort-de-France (for yacht club members)—596-70-26-63.

Puerto Rico

Palmas Sailing Center—809/852-6000, ext. 4498.
Caribbean School of Aquatics—809/723-4740.
Castillo Watersports—809/791-6195.

St. Barthélemy

La Marine Service—590/27-70-34.
Yacht Charter Agency—590/27-62-38.

St. Eustatius

Surfside Statia—800/468-1708.

St. Kitts and Nevis

Kantours—809/465-2098.
Tropical Tours—809/465-4167.

St. Lucia

Brig Unicorn—809/452-6811.
Jacob's Watersports—809/452-8281.
Sailing Bus—809/452-8725.

St. Maarten/St. Martin

Carribbean Watersports—599/5-44387.
Lagoon Cruises & Watersports—599/5-42801.
Turner Watersports—590/87-51-77.

St. Vincent and the Grenadines

Mariner's Watersports—807/457-4228 (St. Vincent).
Sunsports—809/458-3577 (Grenadines).

Trinidad and Tobago

Tobago Marine Sports Ltd.—809/639-0291.

Turks and Caicos

Seatopia—305/442-1396.

U.S. Virgin Islands

Coconut Cruises—809/775-5959 (St. Thomas).
Caribbean Seat Adventures—809/773-5922 (St. Croix).
Mile-Mark Charters—809/773-2285 (St. Croix).
Sea Adventures—809/774-9652 (St. Thomas).
St. John Watersports—809/776-6256 (St. John).
Virgin Islands Charteryacht League—809/774-3944 (St. Thomas).
Watersports Center—809/775-6755 (St. Thomas).

The elegant waterfront villa, called the Coral Seas, near Port Antonio in Jamaica. (*Photo courtesy of Villas and Apartments Abroad*.)

CHAPTER 10

A Villa of Your Own

PICTURE YOURSELF IN this scene: From the spacious veranda, you look out onto the two lovely acres of gardens. Beyond the colorful vegetation is a private, 200-yard beach set on an isolated cove. Off to your left is the private tennis court, its walls of bougainvillaea a riot of color. On the right side of the garden is the small pool next to the beachfront gazebo, a perfect spot for lunch or a dinner by candlelight.

The veranda stretches the full-width of the magnificent three-bedroom house in which you are staying. Calling it a house isn't fair, for inside the 20 French doors opening to the veranda are large elegant rooms fit for an interior decorator's dreams. The rooms—a total of more than 4,000 square feet—are furnished with European antiques, contemporary pieces, fine marble, Dhurrie rugs, and tasteful pastel-colored fabrics. The spacious living room holds comfortable chairs and sofas, a television with a VCR and a complete set of taped movies, stereo, a small library, and, just in case, a Baldwin piano. The dining room is large enough for a dinner party and is furnished nicely with antiques.

The three bedrooms are exquisite. The master bedroom opens onto a separate sitting area on the veranda, while the Peach Room boasts a giant bed and the Mauve Room has twin four-posters. All, of course, have private baths.

Living in such a house would be a lot of work, but not for you, of course. your staff of six will cook, clean, make drinks, tend the garden, find newspapers and tennis rackets, set up beach chairs, serve snacks, and prepare delicious meals. At night, your privacy is ensured by a security guard whose presence on the grounds is protective, but never intrusive.

A fantasy?

No, this is the villa life, and you don't have to be a candidate for the Lifestyles of the Rich and Famous to share it.

What the villas offer is a private lifestyle, quieter and more suited to your tastes than the ambiance found in even the best resorts. What the villas do not have are the lively entertainment found in large resorts, active water sports programs, and constant whirls of people.

The price, you will find, is surprisingly reasonable, considering what you get. For $1,000 a week and up, you can rent a villa in the islands. What you get for the price is usually a one- or two-bedroom villa, with a pool and a maid.

For more money, you get a larger house and a staff to run it, a private beach and tennis court, and occasionally a driver.

The villa described here is "Tranquility Villa," a fabulous oceanfront house on Jamaica about 30 minutes west of Montego Bay. It rents for about $5,000 a week in the winter high season to about half that during the low season. That figure doesn't include food (about $100 per guest per week) and alcohol, gratuities, or a driver (though one is available for hire). To rent it call Villas and Apartments Abroad Ltd. (212/759-1025 or 800/433-3020).

Figure it out for yourself: $5,000 divided by three couples equals $1,666 per couple, a reasonable rate for a villa that was so beautiful that it seemed as if we were staying on the set of a romance movie.

Finding a Villa

There are a number of agencies that rent villas and apartments in the islands. Here is a breakdown by islands of the companies. Call yourself or have your travel agent contact the company.

Anguilla

Jean Browne's Villa World—484 Bloomfield Ave., Suite 24, Montclair, NJ 07042 (201/783-8833 and 800/843-5680).

LaCURE Villas—11661 San Vicente Blvd., Suite 1010, Los Angeles, CA 90049.—(800/387-2726 and from Canada, 800/387-1201).

Prestige Villas—P.O. Box 1046, Soutport, CT 06490 (800/336-0080 and in Connecticut, 203/254-1302).

Property Real Estate Management Services—Box 256, George Hill, Anguilla, British West Indies (809/497-2596).

WIMCO—P.O. Box 1461, Newport, RI 02840 (401/849-8012 and 800/932-3222).

Antigua

Jean Browne's Villa World—484 Bloomfield Ave., Suite 24, Montclair, NJ 07042 (201/783-8833 and 800/843-5680).

Caribbean Home Rentals—P.O. Box 710, Palm Beach, FL 33480 (305/833/4454).

LaCURE Villas—11661 San Vicente Blvd., Suite 1010, Los Angeles, CA 90049 (800/387-2726 and from Canada, 800/387-1201).

Aruba

There are few villas for rent on the island.

Bahamas

Travel Resources—P.O. Box 1043, Coconut Grove, FL 33133 (305/444-8583 and 800/327-5039).

Barbados

Beyond the Blue—Willie Hassell, Black Rock. St. Michael Parish, Barbados (809/424-1808).

Jean Browne's Villa World—484 Bloomfield Ave., Suite 24, Montclair, NJ 07042 (201/783-8833 and 800/843-5680).

Caribbean Home Rentals—P.O. Box 710, Palm Beach, FL 33480 (305/833-4454).

LaCURE Villas—11661 San Vicente Blvd., Suite 1010, Los Angeles, CA 90049 (800/387-2726 and from Canada, 800/387-1201).

Prestige Villas—P.O. Box 1046, Southport, CT 06490 (800/336-0080 and in Connecticut, 203/254-1302).

Travel Resources—P.O. Box 1043, Coconut Grove, FL 33133 (305/444-8583 and 800/327-5039).

Bermuda

Bermuda Department of Tourism—Global House, 43 Church St., Hamilton HM 12, Bermuda, 800/223-6106; 800/223-6107 from New York; 416-923-9600 from Canada. The board has a guide to the many elegant guest houses and other accommodations on the island.

Bonaire

Carib Vacations Ltd.—800/666-8016.

British Virgin Islands

Prestige Villas—P.O. Box 1046, Southport, CT 06490 (800/336-0080 and in Connecticut, 203/254-1302).

Travel Resources—P.O. Box 1043, Coconut Grove, FL 33133. (305/444-8583 and 800/327-5039).

Cayman Islands

Cayman Rent a Villa—Box 681, Grand Cayman, WI (809/947-4144).

Reef House Ltd. Property Management—Box 1540, Grand Cayman, WI (809/949-7093).

Travel Resources—P.O. Box 1043, Coconut Grove, FL 33133 (305/444-8583 and 800/327-5039).

Curaçao

Caribbean Home Rentals—P.O. Box 710, Palm Beach, FL 33480 (305/833-4454).

Dominica

There are few villas and private houses to rent on the island.

Dominican Republic

Travel Resources—P.O. Box 1043, Coconut Grove, FL 33133 (305/444-8583 and 800/327-5039).

Grenada

Caribbean Home Rentals—P.O. Box 710, Palm Beach, FL 33480 (305/833-4454).

Grenada Property Management—Melville Street, St. Georges, Grenada (809/440-1896).

Guadeloupe

Jean Browne's Villa World—484 Bloomfield Ave., Suite 24, Montclair, NJ 07042 (201/783-8833 and 800/843-5680).

Gites de France—590/82-09-30.

Jamaica

Jean Browne's Villa World—484 Bloomfield Ave., Suite 24, Montclair, NJ 07042 (201/783-8833 and 800/843-5680).

LaCURE Villas—11661 San Vincente Blvd., Suite 1010, Los Angeles, CA 90049 (800/387-2726 and from Canada, 800/387-1201).

Prestige Villas—P.O. Box 1046, Southport, CT 06490 (800/336-0080 and in Connecticut, 203/254-1302).

Travel Resources—P.O. Box 1043, Coconut Grove, FL 33133 (305/444-8583 and 800/327-5039).

Villas and Apartments Abroad Ltd.—420 Madison Ave., New York, NY 10017 (212/759-1025 and 800/433-3020).

World Pass Villas—404/876-4966 and 8700/331-8681. (Phone inquiries only.)

Martinique

Villa Rental Service—Operated by the Martinique Tourist Office, Blvd. Alfassa, Fort-de-France, Martinique, FWI. (596/63-79-60).

Puerto Rico

Prestige Villas—P.O. Box 1046, Southport, CT 06490 (800/336-0080 and in Connecticut, 203/254-1302).

St. Barthélemy

SIBARTH—590/27-62-38.

Prestige Villas—P.O. Box 1046, Southport, CT 06490 (800/336-0080 and in Connecticut, 203/254-1302).

Travel Resources—P.O. Box 1043, Coconut Grove, FL 33133 (305/444-8583 and 800/327-5039).

WIMCO—P.O. Box 1461, Newport, RI 02840. (401/849-8012 and 800/932-3222).

St. Eustatius

There are very few rental properties on the island.

St. Kitts and Nevis

St. Kitts Tourist Board—Box 132, Basseterre, St. Kitts (809/465-4040). The board has lists of rental properties.

St. Lucia

Jean Browne's Villa World—484 Bloomfield Ave., Suite 24, Montclair, NJ 07042 (201/783-8833 and 800/843-5680).

Caribbean Home Rentals—P.O. Box 710, Palm Beach, FL 33480 (305/833-4454).

LaCURE Villas—11661 San Vicente Blvd., Suite 1010, Los Angeles, CA 90049 (800/387-2726 and from Canada, 800/387-1201).

Travel Resources—P.O. Box 1043, Coconut Grove, FL 33133 (305/444-8583 and 800/327-5039).

St. Maarten/St. Martin

Jean Browne's Villa World—484 Bloomfield Ave., Suite 24, Montclair, NJ 07042 (201/783-8833 and 800/843-5680).

Jane Condon Corp.—211 E. 43rd St., New York, NY 10017 (212/986-4373).

LaCURE Villas—11661 San Vincente Blvd., Suite 1010, Los Angeles, CA 90049 (800/387-2726 and from Canada, 800/387-1201).

Prestige Villas—P.O. Box 1046, Southport, CT 06490 (800/336-0080 and in Connecticut, 203/254-1302).

Travel Resources—P.O. Box 1043, Coconut Grove, FL 33133 (305/444-8583 and 800/327-5039).

WIMCO—P.O. Box 1461, Newport, RI 02840 (401/849-8012 and 800/932-3222).

St. Vincent and the Grenadines

Jean Browne's Villa World—484 Bloomfield Ave., Suite 24, Montclair, NJ 07042 (201/783-8833 and 800/843-5680).

Mustique Company—Mustique, St. Vincent, W.I. (809/458-4621). (For those whose fantasy is to sleep in Princess Margaret's house).

Trinidad and Tobago

Caribbean Home Rentals—P.O. Box 710, Palm Beach, FL 33480 (305/833-4454).

Turks and Caicos

Travel Resources—P.O. Box 1043, Coconut Grove, FL 33133 (305/444-8583 and 800/327-5039).

U.S. Virgin Islands

Jean Browne's Villa World—484 Bloomfield Ave., Suite 24, Montclair, NJ 07042 (201/783-8833 and 800/843-5680).

LaCURE Villas—11661 San Vicente Blvd., Suite 1010, Los Angeles, CA 90049 (800/387-2726 and from Canada, 800/387-1201).

Prestige Villas—P.O. Box 1046, Southport, CT 06490 (800/336-0080 and in Connecticut, 203/254-1302).

Travel Resources—P.O. Box 1043, Coconut Grove, FL 33133 (305/444-8583 and 800/327-5039).

WIMCO—P.O. Box 1461, Newport, RI 02840 (401/849-8012 and 800/932-3222).

The empire may have slowly vanished into the sunset of history, but the British tradition of high tea lives on some of the islands.

These teas are quite similar to those served in Britain, often including the same scones, finger sandwiches, tea cakes, puff pastries, and a selection of teas. Some inns add an island touch, such as nutmeg cookies, fruit scones with guava jelly, or cakes spiced with local fruits. In many cases, the tea is served on a terrace overlooking the sea. Try these teas for a break from the sun:

Antigua. *Inn at English Harbour, Jumby Bay.*

Bahamas. *Le Meridien Royal Bahamian, Graycliff Hotel and the Ocean Club.*

Barbados. *Glitter Bay, Royal Pavilion and Sandy Lane.*

Bermuda. *Newstead*

British Virgin Islands. *Guana Island Club.*

Jamaica. *Tryall Golf, Tennis and Country Club and the Trident Villas and Hotel.*

Nevis. *All the inns on the island serve tea.*

St. Kitts. *Rawlins Plantation and Golden Lemon.*

St. Lucia. *Cunard La Toc Hotel.*

The Jaragua Resort, Casino and European Spa in Santo Domingo pampers its guests with luxury.

CHAPTER 11

Special Tours, Spas, and Schools

THE ISLANDS OFFER far more than just sand, sun, and rum punches. They are filled with art, archeological finds, and countless varieties of flowers, animals, and birds.

Enjoying these aspects of the islands usually requires that you join a group. Contact these groups for their current schedule of trips, and then enjoy a very different vacation.

Special Tours

The Foundation for Field Research, a California non-profit group, organizes teams of volunteers/tourists to assist scientists in research on the islands.

Recent subjects explored included primate research and observation, searching for Columbus's landing site, and archeological excavations of prehistoric sites in Grenada.

The tax-deductible contribution (usually $1,000 to $1,500 per person) to the foundation covers most on-island expenses such as meals and lodging, but not transportation from the mainland and back nor regular tourist expenses like sightseeing, souvenirs, etc.

Contact: The Foundation for Field Research, 787 South Grade Rd., Alpine, CA 92001 (619/445-9264).

Earthwatch, a Massachusetts-based conservation group, uses volunteers to assist in field research in the areas of marine studies, social sciences, archeology, and art. Trips cost about $1,500 per person.

Recent expeditions included archeological digs at a nineteenth-century fort in Bermuda, a study of the reef life, and a project researching the life of slaves on Montserrat.

Contact: Earthwatch, 680 Mount Auburn St., Box 403, Watertown, MA 02272 (617/926-8200).

The National Audubon Society schedules cruises aboard the *M.S. Polaris* to explore the flora and fauna of Trinidad, Tobago, Bonaire, Aruba, and other islands. The trips cost about $2,400 to $4,000 per person.

Contact: National Audubon Society, Travel Department, 950 Third Ave., New York, NY 10022 (212/832-3200).

The National Trust for Historic Preservation plans tours emphasizing the architecture and history of various islands based aboard the *Sea Cloud* cruise ship. The trips cost $4,000 and up.

Contact: National Trust for Historic Preservation, Special Programs, 1785 Massachusetts Ave., Washington, DC 20036 (202/673-4000).

Oceanic Society Expeditions, an environmental group, leads tours to study marine and coral life. Good swimmers only.

Contact: Oceanic Society Expeditions, Fort Mason Center, Bldg. E, San Francisco, CA 94123 (415/441-1106).

The Smithsonian National Associates Program, a division of the Smithsonian Institution, conducts trips to the islands throughout the year with such subjects as art, culture, history, and bird-watching. The prices start at approximately $2,000 per person.

Contact: The Smithsonian National Associate Travel Program, 1100 Jefferson Dr. SW, Washington, DC 20560 (202/357-4700).

The Sierra Club, a wilderness and conservation group, offers trips exploring reefs and ruins, as well as bicycling and kayaking expeditions. The prices start about $500 and up.

Contact: Sierra Club, Outing Department, 730 Polk St., San Francisco, CA 94109 (415/776-2211).

Fits Equestrian of California conducts horseback tours of Jamaica.

Contact: Fits Equestrian, 2011 Alamo Pintado Rd., Solvang, CA 93463 (805/688-9494).

The World Wildlife Fund takes volunteers on trips studying the environment and conservation in the islands.

Contact: World Wildlife Fund, 1250 24th St. NW, Washington, DC 20037 (212/778-9597).

Schools

The St. Barts Cooking School offers week-long courses on French cuisine. Chef Hubert, holder of a Michelin star for his Bistro Hubert in Paris in the 1970s and 1980s, teaches the courses at the superb Hotel Manapany during the high season.

The five three-hour classes, limited to 20 students, are built around menu planning and preparation of the food. An appetizer, entreé, and dessert are created at each session, and then sampled with the appropriate wines.

The cost is about $1,000 per person, about $1,800 for a couple. That does not include airfare, hotel, or other meals, though packages are available.

Contact: St. Barts Cooking School, 115 Mason St., Greenwich, CT 06830 (203/622-8684).

Spas

Get fit at the following spas:

L'Aqualigne at Pelican Resort—Packages offering weight-loss, anti-cellulite programs, fitness, and beauty. Pelican Key, St. Maarten. 800/223-9815 (212/840-6636).

Leyritz Plantation Hotel & Health Spa—Week-long spa packages include aerobics, walks, hydrotherapy, mud and herbal packs. Basse-Point, Martinique. 800/366-1510 (212/477-1600).

Charlie's Spa at the San Souci Hotel and Club—Six-night spa package includes aerobics, massage, beauty treatment, two-mile walks, and other health-oriented activities. Ocho Rios, Jamaica (800/237-3237 or 305/666-3566).

Hotel Manapany—Exercise programs and beauty and health therapies, including acupuncture, reflexology, and vertabrae therapy. St. Barts (800/847-4249).

Jaragua Resort, Casino and European Spa—Exercise equipment, aerobics classes, yoga and meditation, massages, beauty treatments, diet and fitness consultations. Santo Domingo, Dominican Republic (800/331-3542 or 212/921-0613).

Palmas del Mar—"Wellness Center" offers an analysis of the state of your health, plus aerobics, exercise equipment, aqua aerobics, and yoga. Palmas del Mar, Puerto Rico (800/221-3200).

Parador Baños de Coamo—Hot springs therapy at a lovely country inn. Coamo, Puerto Rico (800/443-0266).

Royal Bahamian Hotel—Packages include fitness classes, mud baths, dance exercise, aerobics, massage, and diet and fitness counseling. Nassau, Bahamas. (800/822-4200).

El San Juan Hotel—Spa offers exercise equipment, massages, jogging course, weight-loss programs, scrubs, beauty treatments, and more. San Juan, Puerto Rico (800/468-8588).

Sonesta Beach Hotel and Spa—Packages built around low-calorie diets, daily exercise, and classes in nutrition, stress, body awareness, and makeup. Southampton, Bermuda (800/343-7170 or 617/576-5947).

Spa Caribe at the Hyatt Regency Cerromar Beach Golf and Tennis Resort—Packages include herbal wraps, exercise, body analysis, aerobics and exercise programs. Dorado, Puerto Rico (800/228-9000).

CHAPTER 12

Ways and Means

BEFORE THE TWO of you pack your sun block, swimsuit, and shades and rush off to the airport for the first flight to an island, a few words of advice are in order.

Getting There

The air transportation system to the Caribbean, Bahamas, and Bermuda has undergone numerous changes in the past year. New routes have been added, new airlines are flying to the islands, and fewer direct flights are now scheduled.

Part of this is the result of airline deregulation, and part is the fallout from Eastern Airlines's labor troubles that forced cuts and changes in their flight schedules.

Wherever you decide to go, you will need a travel agent. This will not cost any extra money, and it might even save a few dollars.

Select one that advertises its experience with booking trips to the islands. If the agents there don't seem to know as much as you after reading this book, try another agency. A knowledgeable agent will save you time, trouble, and money.

Next, when you go is important, for you can save a lot of money off the high-season rates cited in this book. The savings will come not only on rooms, but also on air fares and meals.

The high season in the Caribbean traditionally is from December 15 through April 15. Rates then are 25 percent to 40 percent higher than in the summer months, June through August. The "shoulder" season in the Spring and Fall offers smaller savings.

On Bermuda, the high season is from May through November, when rates run about a third higher than during the cooler winter months of January and February. From Thanksgiving to Christmas and from March through April, the weather is springlike, but the rates remain lower.

In the Bahamas, there isn't an off season. The winter months are popular, though the nights can be chilly and an occasional front comes through sending temperatures on the northernmost islands down to tourist-shocking levels.

Finally, no matter the season, the resorts listed in this book are popular and are often booked for peak weeks as far ahead as a year. In the high season, guests checking out at Barbados' Glitter Bay, for example, make reservations for the same week or weeks a year ahead.

Still, you can get in if you are patient. Be flexible, book early, and if you don't get into the resort of your choice, plan your trip a bit further ahead next time.

Getting Around on the Islands

We have done it every way possible: buses, rental cars, and cabs with tour guides as drivers. By far, the best is by hiring a cab and driver for the day.

The problem with buses is that schedules are nonexistent, stops seem whimsical and crowding doesn't come close to describing the body-to-body arrangement on some of the carriers. The guided tour buses on larger islands, however, are the exception.

We have tried renting a car and have yet to have a good experience. Roads are usually bad, poorly lit at night and rarely marked. Road maps also are a precious commodity, offering only a vague guide on how to get from "A" to "B."

On many islands, you must drive on the left. This means the driver sits on the right and shifts with his or her left hand, which usually requires some adjustment in body/brain communication. Whoever drives is too busy remembering to keep on the left, dodge the potholes, and swerve around chickens, goats, and other obstacles to actually see the passing scenery.

Finally, the cars are just too expensive.

The best option, we finally accepted reluctantly, was to hire a cab and driver for the day. The drivers know how to get around the island, know much about the history, color, and gossip and can even take you to places that aren't in the guides.

Of Rental Cars and Wandering Cows

Driving on the islands often means taking your life in your hands, for you must cope with many things drivers on the mainland rarely see; cows, for instance.

During one visit to Jamaica, we rented a car and toured the island during the day. The only hazards we encountered during the daytrip were the usual: cars parked in the middle of the highway, giant potholes, poorly marked roads, pedestrians walking on the road, and wandering goats.

At night, while driving to a restaurant in the hills above Montego Bay, we encountered an obstacle that made us swear off rental cars.

It was raining lightly, and we were trying to cope with the lack of street lights, street signs, and other accepted risks when we almost had an accident with a large, brown, slowly moving object: a cow.

We swerved around the wandering beast and continued on, almost hitting another cow wandering unattended farther along the road.

The next day, after returning the car, we caught a taxi and decided to ask the driver about the wandering cows.

"What's the story about the cows on the roads at night," we asked. "Isn't that dangerous, for drivers and the cows?"

"Yes, it is a problem," he said. This shocked us. "No problem," is the standard response to any tourist complaint or request. "The owners let the cows wander to feed at night," the driver continued. "Sometimes they don't come back. It is a problem."

On most of these islands, you can tour all the sights in a day or so of driving. We recommend that you take the cab, sit back, and enjoy the sights.

Culture Shock

While you tour the island, you may come across some scenes that will shock first-time visitors to the Caribbean. Many of the islands are very poor and many of their residents live in shacks that would be condemned in the states. It is a fact of life in the Caribbean. If it really bothers your conscience, stay near your resort and don't visit the countryside.

On some islands, ganja (the potent local marijuana) is commonly grown, smoked, and sold. Don't be tempted to buy from the local beach and street entrepreneurs. If you get caught the penalties are harsh and the vendor may be the one to turn you in.

Another cultural change you will notice is the food on the islands. It is often more spicy than dishes served on the mainland, and flying fish and goat are not usually found in the aisles of Safeway. Still, don't fear to try the local West Indian dishes. They are spicy, but far more interesting and delicious than many of the mediocre attempts to imitate continental cuisine.

Finally, do not wear swimsuits and skimpy attire on the streets in town, in shops, or restaurants. On most islands the residents are conservative and very moral. The sight of half-naked bodies walking around may offend.

Be Prepared

You don't need immunizations to visit these islands, but you may want to be careful to drink only the water at the resorts and bottled water elsewhere.

Mosquitoes and other flying insects can be a problem. Carry a good bug repellant with you.

The most common health problem in the islands is severe sunburn. Use a good sunblock and limit your exposure to a few hours a day at first. (We know the latter advice is ridiculous. You paid a lot to get there and no one is going to tell you to get off the beach. Still, it is good advice). If you go sailing, bring tops, hats, and extra lotions, for the sun can be fierce on the ocean.

Bring a small candle, matches, and a flashlight. Power failures are common occurrences on most islands and these items may come in handy if the hotel doesn't provide them.

Never ever expect to buy anything on the island that you can buy first back home. This includes film, batteries, flash bulbs, and medications. These items are occasionally hard to find and are always far more expensive than the price you would pay at home.

The Latest Info

The airports, hotels, and shops offer numerous free guides, magazines and newspapers. Use them. They are excellent sources of information on current events, festivals, new shops, and restaurants.

Final Words

Customs—Regulations vary from island to island and the rules can change at any time. In general, though, you can bring back one liter of alcohol or two bottles of wine plus up to 200 cigarettes duty free. If you exceed these limits, you have to pay a small duty per item.

Shopping—There really aren't any great bargains to be found anymore on the duty-free islands, except for art, crafts, and other local products. The luxury goods—jewelry, crystal, perfume, and china—can often be bought at the same prices at the major discount stores. If you really want to shop for that special watch and bracelet, check prices at your local discounter before you go and then you will have some basis to compare the island prices.

Currency—American dollars, traveller's checks, and credit cards are accepted at most resorts and restaurants. However, using dollars to pay for meals, cabs, and tips isn't the most wise use of your money. Most airports have a change counter. Cash a traveller's check there for the cab fare to the hotel. Then change your checks, if you can, at a local bank rather than the hotel. You will get better rates.

When dealing with cab drivers, always be certain what currency you are talking about when he quotes a fee. If it seems excessive, check with the tourist board, which are often located in airports, for the correct fee.

Always carry about twenty $1 bills for cabs, tips, and other minor expenses in case you cannot change your money into the local currency.

Visas—Island visitors will need a proof of citizenship—a passport, notarized birth certificate, or notarized voter's registration card—and usually a return air ticket to be admitted. We carry passports, which are the best form of identification for cashing traveller's checks.

Tips—Gratuities are an important source of income for the islanders you will come in contact with during your visit. Tip 10 to 15 percent as needed. If you take a picture of an island resident (always ask first), a small tip is usually customary.

On some islands, "service" is added onto the bill at restaurants and hotels. Read the tab carefully and then add onto it if an extra tip is warranted.

INDEX

A

Admiral's House Museum, 47
Albert Lowe Museum, 152
Alcázar de Colón, 13
Altos de Chavón, 14
Androsia Batik Works, 152
Animal Flower Cave, 99
Annandale Falls, 109
Anse du Gouverneur, 64
Antilla, 174
Arawak Indians, 105
Armbister Plantation, 152
Asa Wright Nature Center, 142
Athenry Gardens, 20
Atlantis, 7, 86, 178

B

Bahamas, x, 149–157
Bahia de San Juan, 29
Baie de Fort-de-France, 113
Bailey's Bay, 165
Barbados Wildelife Preserve, 99
Basseterre, 71
Basse-Terre, 58
Basse-Terre Parc Naturel, 58
Bath Hotel, 73
The Baths, 53
Bathsheba, 99
Beaches
  Anse-Mitan, 114
  Anse-Traubaud, 114
  Baie Longue, 78
  Baie Rouge, 78
  Banana Bay, 71
  Blachisseuse Bay, 142
  Blauw Bay, 138
  Boca Chica, 13
  Boca Prince, 130
  Boca Slagbaai, 135
  Browne's Beach, 135
  Buccament Bay, 123
  Cane Garden Bay, 52
  Caravelle Beach, 58
  Carlisle Bay, 47
  Cayman Kai Beach, 6
  Cerro Gordo, 30
  Cocoa Point, 48
  Coki Beach, 86
  Colombier, 64
  Conaree Bay, 71
  Corre Corre Bay, 68
  Cotton Bay, 148
  Cove Bay, 41
  Cupecoy Beach, 78
  Daai Booi Bay, 138
  Dickenson Bay, 47
  Dieppe Bay, 71
  Doctor's Cave Beach, 19
  Eagle Beach, 130
  East End Beach, 6
  Elbow Beach, 165
  Freeman's Bay, 47
  Frigate Bay, 71
  Gande Anse, 110
  Grand Bay, 106
  Greaves End Beach, 99
  Half Moon Bay, 47
  Hawksnest, 87
  Holetown, 99
  Horseshoe Bay, 165
  Isla Verde, 30
  Juan Dolio, 13
  Law Cuevas Bay, 142
  Les Salinas, 114
  Levera Beach, 110
  Long Bay, 47, 52
  Lover's Bay, 143
  Luperón Beach, 14
  Luquitto Beach, 30
  Malendure Beach, 58
  Mallard's Beach, 19
  Manchebo Beach, 130
  Maunday's Bay, 41
  Montego Bay, 19
  Morris Bay, 47

Beaches (*cont.*)
  Mourne Rouge Beach, 110
  Negril Beach, 19
  Oualie Beach, 73
  Palm Beach, 130
  Paqua Bay, 106
  Peel Bay, 165
  Petit Anse de Galet, 64
  Picard Beach, 106
  Pigeon Point, 119
  Pink Beach, 135
  Pinney's Beach, 72
  Playa Grande, 14
  Puerto Plata, 14
  Punta Cana, 13
  Punta Guilarte, 30
  Punta Salinas, 30
  Questelle's Bay, 123
  Raisins-Clairs, 58
  Rendezvous Bay, 41
  Rosada, 30
  Rum Point Beach, 6
  San San Bay, 19
  Santa Barbara Beach, 138
  Seven Mile Beach, 6
  Shoal Bay, 41
  Smoke Alley Beach, 68
  Somerset Long Bay, 165
  Sosúa, 14
  Stone Haven Bay, 143
  Stonehole Bay, 165
  Store Bay, 143
  Tarare, 58
  Trunk Bay, 87
  Turtle Beach, 19
  Vigie Beach, 119
  Warwick Long Bay, 165
  White House Bay, 71
Beef Island, 52
Bequia, 123
Bermuda Aquarium, Museum, and Zoo, 165
Bermuda Arts Centre, 164
Bermuda Perfumery and Gardens, 165
Bermuda reefs, 172
Bianca C., 179
Blue Holes, 152
Blue Mountain, 20
Boggy Peak, 46
Boiling Lake, 105
Bonaire Marine Park, 135
Bordeaux Mountain, 87–88
Botanical Gardens, 123, 151, 164
Bridge House, 165
Bridgetown, 98
Brimstone Hill, 72
Browning, Elizabeth Barrett, 21
Bucco Reef, 143

C

Caguana Indian Ceremonial Park, 30
Careenage, 98
Cariacou, 110
Carib Indians, 105
  reservation, 106
Caribatik, 21
Caribbean, Southern, xi, 129–147
  Aruba, 130–134
  Bonaire, 130–134
  Curaçao, 138–141
  Trinidad and Tobago, 142–147
Carinosa Gardens, 20
Carnival, 142, 144–145
Casa Blanca, 29
Casa del Cordon, 13
Castle Bruce, 106
Castries, 118
Cat Island, 152
Catedral Menor de Santa María, 12
Cathédral de St. Pierre et St. Paul, 59
Cathedral of the Immaculate Conception, 118
Cayman After Dark, 11
Cayman Brac, 6
Cayman Maritime and Treasure Museum, 6
Charlestown, 72
Charlotte Amalie, 3, 84
Christiansted, 88
Cinchona Gardens, 20
Cockpit Country, 20
Columbus, Christopher, 12, 19, 41, 156
Conch Bar Caves, 158
Conord Falls, 109
Cooking Schools, 215–216
Copper and Lumber Store, 47
Coral World, 151
Coral World Marine Park, 86
Craftshouse, 71
Cruise Lines
  Renaissance Cruises, 189–190
  Sea Goddess I, 186–187
  Tall Ship Adventures, 192–193
  Windjammers, 190–192
  Windstar Sail Cruises, 187–189
Cruise Ships,
  Amazing Grace, 191, 192

Fantome, 191, 192
Flying Cloud, 191, 192
Mandalay, 191, 192
Polynesia, 191, 192
Renaissance I–V, 189–190
Sea Goddess I, 184, 186–187
Sir Francis Drake, 192–192
Wind Song, 188
Wind Spirit, 188–189
Wind Star, 187–189
Yankee Clipper, 191–192
Cruises, Day, 197–201
Cruz Bay, 86
Crystal Caves, 165
Culebra, 30
Culture shock, 222–223
Curaçao Seaquarium, 138
Curaçao Underwater Park, 138

D

Deveaux Plantation, 152
Devon House, 21
Devonshire, 164
Diamond Falls and Mineral Baths, 118
Diving/Underwater sightseeing, 174–183
Dominican Convent, 29
Dottin's Reef, 98
Dougalston Estate, 109
Drake's Seat, 85
Dunn's River Falls, 21
Dutch Reform Church, 68

E

Eden Brown Estate, 73
Eight Mile Rock, 151
El Buen Consejo, 174
El Mercada Modelo, 13
El Yunque, 30
Eluthera, 152
Emerald Pool, 105
Empress Josephine, 113
Enterprise, 94, 176

F

Falls of Baleine, 123
Family Islands, 150
Farley Hill, 99
Fête des Cuisiniéres, 59
Fig Tree Drive, 47
Film sites, 43
Flamingo Road, 158
Flower Forest, 98
Folkestone Underwater Park, 98
Fort Ashby, 77
Fort Berkely, 47
Fort Charlotte, 151
Fort Christian, 85
Fort Oranje, 68
Fort-de-France, 113
Frederiksted, 88
Freeport/Lucaya, 151
French Cul de Sac, 79
Fresh Creek, 152

G

Gallery of West Indian Art, 21
George Town, 6
Good Hope, 21
Gouyave, 109
Government House, 85
Grand Bahama, 151
Grand Bahama Museum, 151
Grand Case, 79
Grand Cayman, 6
Grand Etang Lake, 109
Grand-Riviére, 114
Grand-Terre, 58
Great River, 21
Greater Antilles, x–xi, 2–3, 5–37
  Cayman Islands, 6–11
  Dominican Republic, 12–18
  Jamaica, 19–28
  Puerto Rico, 29–37
Green Turtle Cay, 152
Greenwood Great House, 21
Gregory Town, 152
Guana Island, 53

H

Hamilton, Alexander, 72
Harmony Hall, 21
Harrington Sound, 164
Harrison's Caves, 98
Hatchen Bay, 152
Hermitage, 152
High tea, 211
Hispaniola, 12
Honen Dalim, 68

Hospital de San Nicolás de Bari, 15
Hotels
  Abaco Inn, 154
  Admiral's Inn, 49
  Americana Aruba Hotel & Casino, 131
  Anse Chastanet Beach Hotel, 120
  Arnos Vale Hotel, 145
  Asa Wright Nature Center, 143
  Auberge de la Distillerie, 60
  Auberge de la Vielle Tour, 60
  Auberge des Anacardies, 61
  Avila Beach Hotel, 139
  Bavaro Beach Resort, 16
  Biras Creek, 55
  Bitter End Yacht Club, 55
  Blue Horizon's Cottage Hotel, 110
  Blue Waters Beach Hotel, 49
  Blue Waters Inn, 145
  Bluff House Club & Marina, 154
  The Buccaneer, 89
  Calabash, 111
  Caneel Bay, 89–90
  Cap Juluca, 42
  Cap Sud Caraibes, 60
  Cap'n Don's Habitat, 136
  Carambola Beach Resort and Gold Club, 89
  Caravanseri, 79–80
  Caribbean Club, 8
  Casa de Campo, 16
  Castelets, 65
  Cayman Kai, 8
  Charela Inn, 23
  Cinnamon Reef Beach Club, 42
  Club Náutico de Ricón, 33
  Cobbler's Cove Hotel, 107
  Cobblestone Inn, 124
  Coccoloba Plantation, 42
  Colony Club, 101
  Condado Beach Hotel, 32
  Copper and Lumber Store Hotel, 49
  Coral Reef Club, 101
  Coral World Villas, 153
  Cormorant Beach Club, 89
  Cotton Club Bay, 154–155
  The Cotton House, 125–126
  Crane Beach Hotel, 101
  Croney's Old Manor Estate, 75
  Cunard Hotel La Toc and La Toc Suites, 120
  Curaçao Plaza Hotel & Casino, 139
  Curtain Bluff, 49
  Divi Divi Beach Resort, 128, 131
  Divi Flamingo Beach Hotel & Casino, 136
  Divi Tamarijn Beach Resort, 131
  Dorado Naco, 16
  El San Juan Hotel and Casino, 32
  El Sereno Beach Hotel, 65, 66
  Elbow Beach Hotel, 166
  Elysian Resort, 90
  Emerald Valley Resort, 124
  Erebus Inn, 159
  Evergreen Hotel, 107
  Filao Beach Hotel, 65
  Fort Recovery, 54
  François Plantation, 65
  Frangipani Bay Hotel, 125
  Friendship Bay Hotel, 125
  Ginger Bay Beach Club, 101
  Glencoe Harbour Club, 167
  Glitter Bay, 101
  Gobblin Hill, 25
  The Golden Lemon, 74
  Golden Rock, 74
  Golden Tulip Aruba Caribbean Resort & Casino, 131–132
  Golden Tulip Coral Cliff Resort and Beach Club, 130–140
  Grand Anse Hotel, 60
  Grand Lido, 23
  Grand View Beach Hotel, 124
  Graycliff, 156
  Graycliff Hotel, 153
  Green Turtle Club, 154
  Guana Island Club, 56
  Half Moon Golf, Tennis, and Beach Club, 22
  Hamak, 60
  Harbor View, 90
  Hawksbill Beach Hotel, 49
  Hedonism II, 23
  Hevea, 81
  Horizons and Cottages, 167
  Horned Dorset Primavera Hotel, 32
  Horse Shore Beach Hotel, 111
  Hostal Nicolás de Ovando, 15
  Hotel Guanahani, 65
  Hotel Kittina, 159
  Hotel Manapany, 65
  Hotel Normandie, 145
  Hotel Plantation de Leyritz, 115
  Hotel Santo Domingo, 15
  Hotel 1829, 90
  Hyatt Dorado Beach, 33
  Hyatt Regency Cenomar Beach, 33
  Hyatt Regency Grand Cayman, 8–9

Island Reef, 159
Jamaica Inn, 24
Jamaica, Jamaica, 25
Jaragua Resort Hotel, Casino & European Spa, 15
Jumby Bay, 49
L'Habitation, 81
La Bateliére Hotel and Casino, 115
La Belle Creole, 80
La Casa del Frances, 34
La Samanna, 80
La Toubana, 61
Lanata Colony Club, 167
Le Bakoua, 115
Le Méridien Royal Bahamian, 153
Le Meridien Trois-Ilets, 115
Little Dix Bay, 55
Long Bay Beach Resort, 55
Lucayan Beach Resort & Casino, 154
Malliouhana, 42
Manoir de Beauregard, 115
Marigot Bay Resort, 120
Marina Cay Hotel, 56
The Mariners, 43
Mark St. Thomas, 91
Marriott's Castle Harbour Resort, 167
The Meridian Club, 159
Montpelier Plantation Inn, 75
Mt. Irvine Bay Hotel, 145
Nassau Beach Hotel, 153
Newstead, 167
Nisbet Plantation Inn, 75
Ocean Club, 153–154
Olde Yard Inn, 55
OTI Banana Bay Beach Hotel, 74
Oyster Pond Yacht Club, 80
Palm Island Beach Club, 126
Palmas del Mar, 33
Papillote Wilderness Retreat, 107
Parador Banons de Coamo, 33
Parador Hacienda Gripinas, 33
Parador Oasis, 33
Passangrahan Royal Guest House, 80
Pavilions & Pools, 91
Peter Island Hotel and Yacht Club, 55–56
Petit St. Vincent, 124
Pink Beach Club, 167
Pink Sands, 155
Plantation Inn, 24
Playa Chiquita, 16
Point Pleasant, 91
The Princess, 167
Princess Beach Hotel and Casino, 140
Prospect of Whitby Hotel, 160
Prospect Reef, 55
Ramada Gran Hotel el Convento, 32
Rawlins Plantation, 74
The Reefs, 168
The Regency, 157
Reigate Hall, 107
Relais du Moulin, 60–61
Richmond Hill, 23
Round Hill, 23
Royal Pavilion, 102
Runaway Hill, 155
St. Aubin Hotel, 115
St. James Club, 49
St. James Hotel, 111
Salt Raker Inn, 159
Salt Whistle Bay Club, 125
Sandals Negril, 24
Sandy Lane, 102
Sans Souci, 24
Sapphire Beach, 91
Secret Harbor Hotel, 111
Sibony Beach Club, 50
Small Hope Bay Lodge, 154
Sorobon Beach Resort, 136
Southampton Princess, 167
Southern Cross Club, 9
Spice Island Inn, 111
Spring on Bequia, 125
Stonington Beach Hotel, 168
Stouffer's Grand Beach Resort Hotel, 91
Sugar Mill Hotel, 55
Third Turtle Inn, 160
Treasure Island Resort, 9
Tiara Beach Resort, 9
Trident Villas & Hotel, 24
Trinidad Hilton, 145
Tryall Golf, Tennis & Beach Club, 23
Virgin Grand Beach Hotel, 90
Winding Bay Beach Resort, 155
Windjammer Landing, 121
Windmere Island Club, 155
Xanadu Beach & Marine Resort, 154
Young Island, 125

I

Independence Square, 72
Institute of Puerto Rican Culture, 29
Instituto Folklore Bonaire, 135
Isle of Spice, 109

J

Jamaican dishes, 26
Jesus, María y José, 174
Jim Tillet's Art Gallery and Boutique, 85

K

Kingston, 19, 20
Kingstown, 123
Kralendjik, 135

L

La Atarazana, 13
La Bandera, 17
La Casa de los Contrafuertes, 29
La Parguera, 31
La Soufriere, 118
Layou River Valley, 106
Le Morne Rouge, 114
Le Moule, 58
Leeward Islands, xi, 39–95
  Anguilla, 41–45
  Antigua, 46–51
  British Virgin Islands, 52–57
  Guadeloupe, 58–63
  St. Barthélemy, 64–67
  St. Eustatius, 68–70
  St. Kitt's and Nevis, 71–77
  St. Maarten/St. Martin, 78–83
  U.S. Virgin Islands, 84–95
LeLoLai Festival, 35
Les Chutes du Carbet, 58
Les Grand Ballets de Martinique, 117
Les Pitons, 118
Les Trois-Ilets, 113
Lesser Antilles, 3
Little Cayman, 6
Lucayan National Park, 151

M

Maartello Tower and Fort, 48
Macouba, 114
Malecón, 13
Mandinina, 113
Marigot, 79
Marigot Bay, 118
Marina Cay, 54
Marryshow House, 109
Master Shipwright's House, 47
Mayreau, 123
Merengue, 13
Mesopotamia region, 123
Mikveh Israel-Emanual Synagogue, 138
Mimi Bay, 41
Mont Peleé, 113
Montreal Gardens, 123
Morne Diablotin, 106
Mt. Liamuiga, 71
Mountain Top, 85
Mundillo, 30
Museé de la Pagerie, 113
Museé Departementale de Martinique, 113
Musee Vulcanologique, 114
Museum of Antiqua and Barbuda, 46
Museum of Dominican Amber, 14
Museum of Nevis History, 72
Mustique, 124

N

Narrow Straits, 72
Nassau, 151
Nassaustraat, 130
Nelson, Horatio, 46
Nelson, Admiral Lord, 72
Nelson's Dockyard, 46–47
Nevis House of Assembly, 72
Nevis Peak, 72
New Plymouth, 152
New Providence Island, 151
New World Museum of the Sea, 152
Nightspots
  A.J.'s Place, 76
  Alhambra Casino, 133
  Aruba Concorde, 133
  Aruba Dance Theatre, 134
  Aruba Palm Beach Hotel, 134
  Attic, 127
  Autour du Rocher, 67
  Bahamas Princess, 157
  Banana Boat, 161
  Barbados Hilton, 104
  Barbados Horticultural Society, 104
  Black Coral Casino, 137
  Calypso Lounge, 146
  Cap Juluca, 44
  The Casino de Gosier les Bains, 62–63
  Casino de St. François, 63
  Casino Royale, 83
  Casino Trois-Inlets, 117
  The Chips, 51

Cinnamon Reef, 44
Club Calypso, 35
Club Kohuua, 28
Club Scaramouche, 134
Cricket Wicket, 147
Crystal Palace Hotel, 157
Cul de Sac Inn, 44
Cunard Hotel La Toc, 122
Curaçao Caribbean Hotel, 144
Curaçao Plaza Hotel, 141
Divi Little Bay Beach Hotel, 83
E Wowo, 137
Flamingo, 51
Flamingo Beach Hotel, 137
Forty Thieves Club, 170
Gerharts, 137
Golden Tulip, 133
Golden Tulip Las Palmas, 141
Great Bay Beach Hotel, 83
Gros Inlet, 122
Halcyon Cove Resort, 51
Halcyon Wharf Disco, 122
Hyatt Dorado Beach, 35
Hyatt Regency Cerromar, 35
Jaraqua Resort, 18
Kaya Grandi, 137
La Bateliére, 117
La Fiesta, 35
Las Palmas, 18
Le Club, 83
Le New Hippy, 117
Le Privilege, 83
Le Select, 67
Le Sweety, 117
Le Visage, 134
L'Hibiscus, 67
Little Pub, 28
Lucajan Beach Hotel, 157
Mariner's Pub & Bar, 77
Mullet Bay Hotel, 83
Naick's Place, 141
Night Fever, 83
Oasis Club, 179
Paradise Island Cabaret Theater, 157
Pelican Resort, 83
Plantation and Garden Theater, 104
Princess Beach Hotel, 141
Pusser's Landing, 57
Royal Antiguan, 51
Royal St. Kitt's Casino, 76
Rum Runners, 170
St. James Club, 51
St. Maarten Beach Club, 83
Santo Domingo Sheraton, 18
Seaview Hotel, 83
Shirley Heights Lookout, 51
Sir Winston's Reggae Club, 28
Sparrow's Hideaway, 147
Splash, 122
Stellaris Club, 134
Tabora's Restaurant, 104
Treasure Island, 83
Tree House, 28
Tropico, 35
Uprising, 161
Willemstad Room, 141
North Sound, 7
Northwest Reef, 158

O

Ocean Hole, 152
Ocho Rios, 19
Officer's Quarters, 47
Old Gin House, 68
Old Town, 78
Oranjestad, 68, 130

P

Paget, 164
Palm Island, 124
Palmer, Annie, 21
Paradise Island, 151
Paradores, 31
Parc Floral et Culture, 113
Par-La-Ville, 164
Parque de Los Tres Ojos, 14
Perfume Factory, 151
Peter Hughes Dive Center, 9
Peter Island, 53
Petit Martinique, 110
Petit St. Vincent, 126
Phosphorescent Bay, 31
Pico Duarte, 14
Pigeon Island, 58
Pirate's Week, 6
Pissaro, Camille, 85
Planter's punch, 37
Pointe-á-Pitre, 58–59
Ponce de León, Juan, 29
Port Antonio, 19
Port-of-Spain, 142
Potter's Cay, 151
Precautions, 223–224
Puerto Plata, 14

Q

Queen's Park, 98
Queen's Park House, 98
Queen's Park Racetrack, 142
Quill, 68

R

Rand Memorial Nature Center, 151
Red Hook Harbor, 86
Redcliff Quay, 46
Relais Creole, 59
Restaurants
  Admiral's Inn, 50
  Agaye Terrace, 92
  Alcazar, 17
  Almond Tree, 27
  Amadeus, 34
  Auberge de la Vielle Tour, 62
  Auberge de St. François, 62
  Aux Filets Bleus, 116
  Bagatelle Great House, 103
  Bali Floating Restaurant, 132
  Basils Beach Bar, 127
  Beach Terrace Dining Room, 92
  Betty Masioll's Great House, 112
  Bistro des Amis, 137
  Bistro Le Clochard, 140
  Boonoonoonoos, 133
  Café de Sol, 18
  Cafe Martinique, 157
  Café St. Michel, 17
  Café Savanna, 146
  Cafe Valencia, 157
  Carambola, 103
  Caribbean Club, 10
  Casanova, 27
  Castelets, 66
  Chef Tell's Grand Old House, 10
  Chez Clara, 62
  Chez Lafitte, 168
  Chez Mathilde, 132
  Chez Violetta-La Creole, 62
  Clouds, 50
  Coconut's Beach, 112
  The Cook Rum, 10
  The Cooperage, 76
  The Courtyard Terrace, 157
  Daphne's, 127
  De Taveerne, 140
  Den Laman Aquarium Bar & Restaurant, 137
  Diamont Creole, 116
  The Dolphin, 51
  Doras, 161
  El Batey de Tonita, 35
  Ellington's, 92
  Escoffier Room, 157
  Europe Restaurant, 155
  Felix, 82
  Flamingo's, 18
  Fonda de la Atarazana, 17
  Fourways Inn, 169
  François Plantation, 66
  Frangipani, 127
  French Restaurant, 127
  Frigate Bay Beach Hotel, 75
  Frilsham House, 155–156
  Georgian House, 26
  The Georgian House, 76
  Gloriette, 66
  The Golden Lemon, 76
  Gonzalez Seafood, 35
  Green Parrot, 121
  Gregerie East, 92
  Harbor View, 93
  Hermitage, 76
  Hibernia, 44
  The Horned Dorset Primavera, 35
  Hotel 1829, 93
  Il Giardino, 35
  Island Princess, 160
  Island Reef, 160
  Jimmy's, 18
  Johnno's, 44
  Koko's, 103
  La Bahia, 17
  La Balata, 62
  La Belle Creole, 112
  La Belle Epoque, 116
  La Belle France, 82
  La Bistroelle, 140
  La Boucan, 146
  La Cage aux Folles, 103
  La Canne á Sucre, 62
  La Chateau Creole, 103
  La Chaumiere, 34
  La Compostela, 35
  La Crémaillere, 66
  La Dolce Vita, 133
  La Fantasie, 146
  La Fontane, 116
  La Grand 'Voile, 116
  La Maison sur Plage, 69
  La Petit Jardin, 127
  La Provence, 82

La Reina de España, 35
La Residence, 83
La Robe Creole, 107
La Samanna, 82
La Villa Creole, 116
Lanatiana Colony Club, 169
L'Aventure, 50, 82
Le Balisier, 112
Le Barbaroc, 62
Le Bec Fin, 81
Le Bilboquet, 81
Le Chic, 137
Le Marine, 66–67
Le Poisson d'Or, 82
Le Relais, 67
Le Tiffany, 117–118
Le Toque Lyonaisse, 67
L'Escargot, 10, 82
L'Etoille, 69
L'Hibiscus, 66
Les Pitons, 121
Lina, 17
Lucy's, 92
Lucy's Harbour View Restaurant, 44
Mama's, 112
Margaret Rose, 169
Mariner's Inn, 127
Marquerite's, 26
Mesón de la Cava, 17
Mona Lisa Bar & Restaurant, 137
Mrs. Scatliffe's Restaurant, 57
New Harbourfront, 169
Newport Room, 169
Nisbet Plantation Inn, 76
The Norwood Room, 169
Old Donkey Cart House, 146
Old Gin House, 69
Once Upon a Table, 169
The Orchard, 107
Oyster Pont Yacht Club, 82
Palm Terrace, 103
Papagao Restaurant, 133
Papiamento, 132
Papillon's Rendezvous, 160
Papillote Wilderness Retreat, 107
The Patio, 76
Piperade, 103
The Pork Pit, 27
Raffles, 103
Rain, 121
Reigate Hall, 108
Relais du Moulin, 62
Restaurant Ballahou, 67
Rick's Cafe, 21, 27
Rijsstaffel Indonesia Restaurant, 140–141
Ristorante Pappagallo, 10
The Ruins, 27
St. James Hotel, 112
San Antonio's, 121
Sandpiper, 160
Santiago, 34–35
Seashell, 103
Secret Harbour Hotel, 112
Spartaco, 82
Spice Island Inn, 112
Stone Oven Bar & Restaurant, 70
The Sugar Mill, 27
Sugar Mill, 146
Sugar Mill Kitchen, 92
Sugar Mill Restaurant, 57
Sun and . . . , 157
Town House, 27
Turtle Bay Dining Room, 92
Vesuvio, 17–18
Victor's Hide Out, 93
Victor's Hideaway, 76
Wajang Doll, 82
Waterlot Inn, 169
Young Island, 127
Rio Camuy Cave Park, 30–31
R.M.S. Rhone, 53, 176
Road Town, 52
Rose Hall Great House, 21
Roseau, 105
Royal Botanic Gardens, 142
Royal Victoria Gardens, 151

S

Sage Mountain National Park, 52
St. Ann's Harbor, 139
St. Croix, 84
St. François, 58
St. George's, 109
St. George's Anglican Church, 71–72
St. George's Cathedral, 123
St. Jean, 64
St. John's, 46, 84
St. John's Cathedral, 46
St. Mary's Roman Catholic Cathedral, 123
St. Pierre, 113
St. Thomas, 84
Ste. Anne, 58
San Felipe del Morro, 29
San Francisco Monastery, 13
San José Church, 29

San Juan Cathedral, 29
Sandys Parrish, 164
Santa Maria, 12
Santo Domingo, 12
  Colonial Zone, 12
  Columbus Square, 12
  Parque Colon, 12
Santurce District, 30
Saw Pit, 47
Scarborough, 143
Scharbo District, 138
Sea turtles, 87
Shaw Park Botanical Gardens, 20
Shirley Heights, 47
Silver Cay, 151
Simpson Bay Lagoon, 78
Sir Francis Drake Channel, 52
Smith, John, 72
Smith's, 164
Somerset Fall's, 21
Soufriére, 118
Southampton, 161
Spanish Town, 53
Spas, 216–217
Spencer Cameron Art Gallery, 71
Statia Museum, 68
Stavronikita, 175
Stocks and Pillory, 165
Sugarloaf Mountain, 68
Sulphur Springs, 105
Sun Bay, 30

T

Tarpoum, 152
Tongue of the Ocean, 152
Tortola, 52
Tourist Information Centers
  Anguilla, 45
  Antigua and Barbuda, 51
  Aruba, 134
  Bahamas, 157
  Barbados, 104
  Bermuda, 171
  Bonaire, 137
  British Virgin Islands, 57
  Cayman Islands, 11
  Curaçao, 141
  Dominica, 108
  Dominican Republic, 18
  Grenada, 112
  Guadelope, 63
  Jamaica, 28
  Martinique, 117
  Puerto Rico, 36
  St. Barthelemey, 67
  St. Croix, 95
  St. Eustatius, 70
  St. John, 95
  St. Kitt's and Nevis, 77
  St. Lucia, 122
  St. Maarten/St. Martin, 83
  St. Thomas, 95
  St. Vincent and Grenadines, 127
  Trinidad and Tobago, 147
  Turks and Caicos, 161
Tours, 213–215
Trafalgar Falls, 105
Transportation
  on the islands, 220–222
  to the islands, 219–220
Turks and Caicos, x, 149–150, 158–161

V

The Valley, 41
The Valley of Desolation, 105
Vieques, 30
Villas
  rental agencies, 205–210
  Coral Seas, 202
Virgin Gorda, 53
Virgin Gorda Peak, 53

W

The Wall, 152, 158
Warwick, 164
Washington/Slagbaai Park, 135
Waterfort Arches, 138
White River, 21
Wilheminastraat, 130
Willemstad, 138
Windward Islands, xi, 97–127
  Barbados, 98–104
  Dominica, 105–108
  Grenada, 109–112
  Martinique, 113–117
  St. Lucia, 118–122
  St. Vincent and the Grenadine,
    123–127

Y

Yacht Brokers, 197
Yaniqueques, 17